Mud, Sweat and Beers

D1488522

Global Sport Cultures

Eds Gary Armstrong, *University of Reading*, Richard Giulianotti, *University of Aberdeen*, and David Andrews, *The University of Memphis*

From the Olympics and the World Cup to extreme sports and kabaddi, the social significance of sport at both global and local levels has become increasingly clear in recent years. The contested nature of identity is widely addressed in the social sciences, but sport as a particularly revealing site of such contestation, in both industrialising and post-industrial nations, has been less fruitfully explored. Further, sport and sporting corporations are increasingly powerful players in the world economy. Sport is now central to the social and technological development of mass media, notably in telecommunications and digital television. It is also a crucial medium through which specific populations and political elites communicate and interact with each other on a global stage.

Berg publishers are pleased to announce a new book series that will examine and evaluate the role of sport in the contemporary world. Truly global in scope, the series seeks to adopt a grounded, constructively critical stance towards prior work within sport studies and to answer such questions as:

- How are sports experienced and practised at the everyday level within local settings?
- How do specific cultures construct and negotiate forms of social stratification (such as gender, class, ethnicity) within sporting contexts?
- What is the impact of mediation and corporate globalisation upon local sports cultures?

Determinedly interdisciplinary, the series will nevertheless privilege anthropological, historical and sociological approaches, but will consider submissions from cultural studies, economics, geography, human kinetics, international relations, law, philosophy and political science. The series is particularly committed to research that draws upon primary source materials or ethnographic fieldwork.

Previously published title in the Series:

Gary Armstrong and Richard Giulianotti (eds), *Fear and Loathing in World Football*

GLOBAL SPORT CULTURES

Mud, Sweat and Beers
A Cultural History of Sport and Alcohol

Tony Collins and Wray Vamplew

Oxford • New York

First published in 2002 by
Berg
Editorial offices:
150 Cowley Road, Oxford, OX4 1JJ, UK
838 Broadway, Third Floor, New York, NY 10003-4812, USA

Berg is the imprint of Oxford International Publishers Ltd.

Library of Congress Cataloging-in-Publication Data
Collins, Tony.
    Mud, sweat, and beers : a cultural history of sport and alcohol / Tony Collins
and Wray Vamplew.
        p. cm. -- (Global sport cultures, ISSN 1472-2909)
Includes bibliographical references and index.
    ISBN 1-85973-553-3
    1. Athletes--Alcohol use.   2. Drinking of alcoholic beverages--Social aspects.
3. Alcoholic beverage industry.   I. Vamplew, Wray.   II. Title.   III. Series.
    RC1245 .C65 2002
    362.292'088'796--dc21

                                                                    2001008221

British Library Cataloguing-in-Publication Data
A catalogue record for this book is available from the British Library.

ISBN   1 85973 553 3 (Cloth)
         1 85973 558 4 (Paper)

Typeset by JS Typesetting, Wellingborough, Northants.
Printed in the United Kingdom by Biddles Ltd, Guildford and King's Lynn.

Contents

Introduction   1

1   This Sporting House: The Pub and Sport   5

2   A Thirsty Business: The Drinks Industry and Sport   39

3   Cheers! Alcohol and the Sporting Crowd   69

4   A Little of What Does You Good? Alcohol, the
    Athlete and Sporting Performance   91

Conclusion: More than Beer and Skittles?   119

Bibliography   127

Index   139

Introduction

'Football is a fascination of the devil and a twin sister of the drink system,' declared an Anglican vicar in 1893.[1] Although the leisure interests of Satan lie beyond the scope of this work, it is undoubtedly true that football and all other sports have enjoyed a close and familial relationship with alcohol throughout the ages.

Today, hardly a month goes by without the tabloids exposing the drinking habits of a sports star. And barely a day passes without the sight of alcohol sponsorship or advertising at a major sporting event. But while those who believe in a mythical Golden Age of sport may point to such examples as yet more evidence of declining morality or rampant commercialism, in reality they are just the latest stage in the long and symbiotic link between sport and the 'demon drink'. Those who hanker for an alcohol-free golden age of sport should perhaps consider that most sporting trophies are cups, the original idea of which was to facilitate the imbibitions of the winning team or athlete.

This book aims to explore the multi-faceted relationship between alcohol in all its aspects and sport at all levels. Our starting point for this has been to integrate the history of the drinks industry in Britain since the mid-nineteenth century with the history of sport in the same period and trace the story from there.

For both sport and alcohol, the late-Victorian period was one of tremendous and rapid change. The drinks industry underwent a process of consolidation which saw the number of pubs and breweries decline rapidly while alcohol consumption also fell quickly. Mass spectator sports such as football and rugby rose to great prominence in the 1880s and the following decade saw the growth of middle-class sports such as golf and tennis.

We trace the subsequent relationship by looking at four key aspects:

- the role of the pub and its decline as a social centre and conversion into a retail outlet;
- the development of modern marketing techniques by the breweries and the changing ways in which sport was used to sell alcohol;
- the importance of alcohol to the sporting crowd and its relationship to crowd behaviour;

- the changing attitudes to drink as both an aid to and an inhibitor of athletes' sporting performance, together with its role in the life of both elite and recreational sports men and women and its relationship to the lifestyle of the professional athlete.

Additionally, we look at the attitude of the temperance movement towards sport and consider the impact of government legislation on the use of alcohol by sports spectators and participants.

In choosing this structure, we have sought to present a rounded and comprehensive history of the subject. However, this is not to imply that the work is exhaustive; indeed, we hope to have shed light on enough areas to encourage others to illuminate them in far greater detail.

The history of the drinks trade and associated alcohol industries is one which has been well served by historians, such as Peter Mathias, Ian Donnachie, Terry Gourvish and Richard Wilson, yet an examination of the social and cultural role played by alcohol is still underdeveloped. Brian Harrison's ground-breaking 1971 study of the nineteenth-century temperance movement, *Drink and the Victorians*, remains the benchmark for subsequent studies. Paradox-ically, and perhaps inspired by Harrison's work, it is the temperance movement and attempts to restrict the consumption of alcohol which have attracted most attention from scholars.[2]

One of the more notable exceptions to this is Paul Jennings's work on the social and economic history of pubs in Bradford, which demonstrates both the painstaking research needed to develop a convincing portrait of the subject and the insights which such studies can throw on the social development of the wider community.[3] More recently attention has focused on the history of consumption and the social meanings attached to it. John Burnett's *Liquid Pleasures* and Andrew Barr's *Drink: A Social History* have both sought to place alcohol consumption in a broader social context and relate it to the changing work, leisure and cultural patterns of society.[4] It is also important to note that there is a flourishing community of non-academic historians of pubs and breweries, many of whose members have produced important studies on the subject.

There is also of course a significant literature on football hooliganism and drink, which tends to portray the relationship between sport and alcohol as being a question of public order, and an even larger body of work which examines alcohol from the perspective of sports medicine and performance enhancement – some of it eerily reminiscent of the temperance campaign literature of the early twentieth century in its condemnation of its subject.

However, with the single exception of John Weir's 1992 work on drink and early Scottish football, there have been no studies which seek to examine the cultural and social history of the relationship between sport and alcohol in Britain.[5] There are perhaps a number of reasons for this. The relationship appears to be self-evident, a view which could imply that further research is unnecessary. It is also the case that the social history of sport is still in its adolescence and has yet to enjoy the status of other fields of historical research. There is also a tendency to 'compartmentalise' research into discrete areas which rarely impinge on other fields.

In contrast, we hope that this work may help to suggest a shift in the focus of studies of sport and leisure away from such compartmentalised investigations of individual aspects of leisure towards broader, holistic explorations of leisure and recreational histories. The fact that sport and alcohol cross-pollinate with each other in so many ways helps to throw fresh light on both of their histories.

For example, the importance of brewers to commercial sport – financing professional football clubs and their grounds, underwriting golf, cricket and other sports' clubs, and, more recently, providing extensive funds through sponsorship – has been hinted at by scholars but the extent of this relationship has not hitherto been explored.

On a cultural level, the deep and long connections between drinking and sporting enjoyment, whether as a participant or spectator, have been previously acknowledged but, outside of the context of football hooliganism, remain largely uninvestigated. We hope that by highlighting the links between drinking and sport and issues such as masculinity, class and regional identity, we have suggested avenues for future investigations in related fields.

As with all scholarly work, this book could not have been written without the help and advice of many other people. First and foremost we owe a debt of gratitude to the Leverhulme Trust whose support made this research for this work possible. We are also especially grateful to Richard Cox for initially suggesting the topic, Joyce Kay for brain-storming on the grant application, Neil Tranter, Peter Radford, Duncan Stewart, Patrick Chaplin, John Harding, Gordon Taylor of the Professional Footballers' Association, Ken Thomas at the Courage Archives, Alma Topen of the Scottish Brewing Archive, Liz Press of the Bass Museum, Jan Booth of the Brewers and Licensed Retailers Association, Dorothy Sheridan of the Mass-Observation Archive at the University of Sussex, Jed Smith of the Museum of Rugby Union at Twickenham, the staffs of numerous libraries and local archives, the many participants at conferences of sports history organisations in Britain and Europe for ideas raised in response to papers, and particularly our colleagues at the International Centre for Sports History and Culture: Mike Cronin, Richard Holt, Pierre Lanfranchi,

Tony Mason and Matt Taylor. Quotations from the Mass-Observation Archive are reproduced with permission of Curtis Brown Group Ltd, London, on behalf of the Trustees of the Archive and are copyright of the Trustees of the Mass-Observation Archive. Finally, our deepest thanks must go to our respective partners, Cathy France and Janice Vamplew, who have both contributed much work and support in the research and writing of this book.

Notes

1. *Yorkshire Post*, 22 March 1893.
2. Ian Donnachie, *A History of the Brewing Industry in Scotland*, Edinburgh, 1979; T.R. Gourvish and R.G. Wilson, *The British Brewing Industry*, Cambridge, 1994; D.W. Gutzke, *Protecting the Pub: Brewers and Publicans against Temperance*, Woodbridge, 1989; Brian Harrison, *Drink and the Victorians*, 2nd Edition, Keele, 1994; Peter Mathias, *The Brewing Industry in England, 1770–1830*, Cambridge, 1959.
3. Paul Jennings, *The Public House in Bradford, 1770–1970*, Keele, 1995.
4. Andrew Barr, *Drink: A Social History*, London, 1998; John Burnett, *Liquid Pleasures: A Social History of Drinks in Modern Britain*, London, 1999.
5. John Weir, *Drink, Religion and Scottish Football 1873–1900*

1

This Sporting House: The Pub and Sport

In one of its perennial campaigns to highlight the importance of alcohol to the national culture, *The Licensed Trade News* declared proudly in 1910 that 'in all probability no other trade or industry contained within its ranks as great a proportion of athletes as the Licensed Trade'. It is a claim that is hard to refute. Ever since it acquired its distinct identity, the public house has always been closely connected to sport. Whether as an alehouse, a tavern, an inn or a modern pub, sport has been at the heart of its life. And the publican, whether an athlete or not, has been central to the development of sport both ancient and modern.[1]

It is difficult to underestimate the importance of the drinking place to pre-industrial societies. In general, it served as the fulcrum for village life. It was a meeting place for socialising, doing business, finding work, receiving wages and organising political activity. It was a centre for travel, serving as a stopping station for coaches, a stop at which to change horses and a hotel for travellers. It was the focus for leisure activities for the whole community, encompassing everything from organising annual fairs and feasts to arranging informal singing and dancing. Most importantly, it was a place in which to drink alcohol, an activity which was a form of leisure in itself.

Certainly by the sixteenth century, and probably much earlier, the ale house was the main arena for staging sports events, as landlords found that the space adjoining their property could be utilised to promote sports events which would attract crowds. The yards, greens and grounds of the drinking place provided the spaces in which sports as diverse as skittles, quoits, bowls, boxing, wrestling, tennis, foot-racing, cricket and any number of activities featuring animals could be staged. In order to organise events which would bring in a bigger clientele, the publican became the promoter of sports, arranging matches and providing prize money, as well as being the bookmaker. If there was money to be made from the ale and food consumed by the sporting crowd, the same was true of the opportunities for gambling.

Saint Monday, the custom by which workers stayed away from work on Mondays to pursue their leisure activities, was sustained by the pub providing not only the ale which was so important to the tradition but also the entertainment, whether it be organised commercially, such as bull- or badger-baiting, or informally, such as cards or bowls. And, as the traditional rural structure of society declined in the early nineteenth century, the pub retained its importance for the mass of the population crowded into the newly industrialising cities. It was now an oasis of warmth and conviviality in a cold and harsh world, a temporary escape from the grind of the factory and the inadequacies of the home. For the working classes, it was also, barring the occasional intrusion from the local constabulary, a world apart from and free of their social superiors; little changed in this aspect of pub life up until the First World War, as Robert Roberts remarked about Edwardian Salford: 'To the great mass of manual workers the local public house spelled paradise . . . After the squalor from which so many men came there dwelt within a tavern all one could crave for.'[2]

Drinking places were not only important for the recreation of the lower classes; they were also centres for the recreation of the higher echelons of society. They possessed their own social hierarchy, with large, ornate coaching houses having a higher social standing than the lowly village ale house. The elite cricket teams and coaching clubs of the late eighteenth century often took their names from hostelries. Hunts and point-to-point races usually began and/or finished at inns. Horse racing was a sport in which all classes mixed and in which the pub played a central role; for example, Thomas Coleman, landlord of St Albans' Turf Hotel, organised the first modern steeplechase in 1830. Publicans organised races, provided refreshment tables and booths and arranged other attractions for the assembled racegoers: cock-fighting was regularly staged at pubs to coincide with horse racing to provide sport and gambling opportunities before, during and after race meetings. By 1853 Stirling Races was hosting 'The Stirling Innkeepers' Stakes' and by the 1860s races organised outside of the traditional courses became disparagingly know as 'publicans' races'. But, as the gentry's patronage of rural sports began to fall away at the end of the eighteenth century, the landlord rose to a position unrivalled in its importance to the promotion of sport.

The deep bonds between the pub and sport can be seen in pub names and their signs. Pub signs often reflect the way of life, both past and present. Thus they may offer clues to the sporting connections of the public house in a particular locality. Yet care has to be taken in their interpretation as not all are what they might seem, the bestiary especially. Many bears, boars, bulls, falcons, greyhounds and hawks are representative of the coats-of-arms of local nobility rather than animals of sport. Cock Inns might indicate fighting cocks or the provision of cockshying, but could also refer to the spigot on a barrel of ale or even have religious connotations. Geographical semantics mean that Bull is sometimes indicative of the French port of Boulogne – as in Bull and Mouth for the entry to the town's harbour – rather than the animal subjected to baiting. Research at the local level clearly is needed before any dogmatic assertions can be made as to the origin and meaning of any particular sign.[3]

That said, it is reasonable to assume that many signs do have a sporting connection, existing historically as advertisements of what might be provided by the landlord and today serving as a reminder of sporting times gone by. Popinjays or Parrots were targets on the butts behind the inns; Bears – black or brown, upright or on all fours – often suggested the existence of a bear pit where the beasts were whipped or baited; and the Fox and Hounds public houses were as ubiquitous in hunting country as were the Greyhound variety around northern coursing grounds. Animal sports with dogs feature extensively on signboards, though caution still has to be exercised. The Talbot was a large hunting dog, but it could also honour the House of Talbot (the Earls of Shrewsbury).[4] The ground is more certain when the dog appears in combination with other animals that it baited, hunted or collected for its shooter master. One of these, the Dog and Duck, occasionally refers to fowling but more generally to the use of dogs, spaniels in particular, to hunt a duck, its wings pinioned and its only means of escape being to dive to the bottom of the pond owned by the landlord providing the sport. The largest of these in London was the several acres of water kept by innkeeper Mr Ball, now remembered in the name Balls Pond Road. The last one to survive in the very heart of the city was within 50 yards of Bond Street, commemorated as Ducking Pond Mews.[5]

It is also the case that many sports-related pub names are a relatively recent innovation, often the product of brewery marketing managers' imaginations rather than a long history of involvement with sport. Barrie Cox records that the first sport-related pub name was the Horse & Jockey in Uppingham, Rutland in 1783, followed by Crickets in 1804 and Hare & Hounds in 1817. This is probably a later time-frame than other historians would accept; in 1757 the first recorded game of cricket in Yorkshire was played at the Bowling Green Inn in Chapel Allerton in Leeds, and the popularity of bowling greens in pubs would suggest that the name has a long history, for no other reason that the name served to advertise a significant facility of the pub. Certainly sport-related names were a small minority of pub names in the nineteenth century. For example, of 447 pubs and beer houses in the Halifax area in 1871, only twenty-six, or just under 6 per cent had names that could be directly related to sport. Other than those with the word sportsman in the title, the names related to horse racing, or hunting. Similarly a survey of pubs in Huddersfield throughout the 1890s shows that only five of 192 pubs had sport related names, again relating to horses and hunting.[6]

As with much of pre- and early-industrial leisure, animals provided much of the focus for pub entertainment, a staple being provided by the hunting and killing instincts of dogs. Bull- and bear- and occasionally ape-baiting were common sights at fairs and fêtes and their staging was a feature of pubs large enough to house bull or bear pits. Nor were these the only animals to suffer in this way. Badgers and ducks were often the target for dogs – duck-baiting was reputed to be one of the favoured sports of Charles II.

As can be seen in the names of many modern pubs, and also in the trade logo of the Courage brewing group, cock fighting was one of the most popular of the sports connected to the drinks trade. It fitted perfectly with the needs of the publican: matches were simple to arrange, the pits in which the cocks fought were small and easy to construct and, most importantly of all, it allowed maximum scope for gambling. Cockfights could be arranged as entertainment in themselves or as attractions to entice visitors for other local events such as horse racing or fairs. Although 'Stow's Survey' in 1720 had associated cock-fighting and 'lying at alehouses,' with 'the lower classes', the sport also drew considerable support from the more sports-minded of the aristocracy.[7] Reput-edly the last great cockfight before Parliament outlawed it in 1849 took place in a pub in Lincoln between birds belonging to Lord Derby and a breeder named Gilliver for a total stake of 12,000 guineas. The commoner won.[8]

The support of the aristocracy and the gentry for such sports had however begun to fade even before the stricter moral codes of industrial society had been codified in the ban of 1849, making the publican the most important factor in their survival and promotion. The decline and eventual banning of cockfighting was accompanied by a concomitant rise in the popularity of ratting, a sport whereby dogs would catch and kill rats in a confined space either inside the pub or within its grounds. Huge numbers of rats were disposed of in this way – a London publican in the 1820s boasted that he had acquired 26,000 rats in one year to fuel this entertainment – and the better, or most savage, dogs could catch over 100 rats in around fifteen minutes.[9]

Other than those involving animals, no sport had closer links with the pub than boxing. From its earliest times, prizefighting was heavily dependent on the support of the publican for its promotion, its staging and its admin-istration. Landlords gave prize money, held stakes and took bets; they provided the ring for the boxers, refreshments for the audience and publicity for the fight and its aftermath. The illegality of prizefighting, the uneven enforcement of which was dependent upon the prevailing climate of public opinion, the nature of the magistrates in the area and possible threat of public disorder, meant that formal organisation of the sport was almost impossible, giving the publican an importance unequalled in other sports.

And, of course, as was pointed out by many commentators of the time, today's fighter was merely tomorrow's publican in waiting. When their careers in the ring ended, many prizefighters took up the tenancy of a pub, often having the licence bought for them through collections from admirers. The first, suggests Dennis Brailsford, was Peter Corcoran who took over the Blakeney's Head in St Giles in the 1780s.[10] Tom Spring's The Castle in Holborn became a centre not just for boxing but for London sporting activity in general. Jack Randall, a lightweight champion of the 1820s, gained a marginally more lasting fame when he retired to take over a pub which became the subject of Hazlitt's famous essay *The Fight*. Pierce Egan listed twenty-six 'Sporting Houses' in 1821 and twenty-nine in 1829 which were 'kept by pugilists and other persons connected with the sporting world respecting pugilism'.[11] By the 1840s, dozens of London pubs were known as boxing pubs, many hosted by ex-pugilists and the unofficial headquarters of the sport moved from pub to pub as the standing of their landlords waxed and waned in the prizefighting universe.

But although prizefighting was predominantly concentrated in London, pubs in other areas of the country also had strong traditions in the sport. By 1868 *Fistiana* listed 114 pubs across England which were known as being prizefighting pubs, covering London, Birmingham, Sheffield, Derby, Manchester, Liverpool and the Potteries.[12] The George at Odiham in Hampshire was the stage for contests for over 300 years from 1547. The Ram Jam Inn at Stretton near Grantham hosted Tom Cribb's 1810 eight-round victory over American Tom Molyneaux, after which he retired as the All-England Champion Boxer and bought the Union Arms off London's Haymarket, a pub which today bears his name. The Fountain Inn at Tipton in the West Midlands was the base for William Perry, 'The Tipton Slasher', who himself eventually became a publican in the town. Sadly it was also the case that many ex-pugilists were quickly to become ex-publicans: Jem Belcher's time at the Jolly Brewer in Wardour Street led to his death as an alcoholic aged just thirty.

As prizefighting fell into decline and disrepute from the 1860s, eventually to be replaced by gloved boxing under the Marquis of Queensbury rules, the 'manly art' was kept alive by the boxing pubs dotted around the capital which offered instruction, sparring contests and exhibitions by resident fighters. By the turn of the century, nostalgia for the golden age and great names of prizefighting had become a cottage industry in itself, with books, prints and newspaper articles galore celebrating the inextricable link between the sport and the pub.[13]

Although seemingly in contrast to the violence associated with most pub sports, cricket too was very much the child of the drinking house. The first known publication of the laws of the game was the 1755 'New Articles of the Game of Cricket', subtitled 'Particularly That of the Star & Garter in Pall Mall', which were drawn up by the gentlemen involved in London's leading cricket clubs. John Nyren, the chronicler of the sport's infancy, was the landlord at Hambledon's Bat and Ball Inn, which also served as the village side's pavilion and club house. Visitors to Thomas Lord's original cricket ground were greeted by an advertisement for wines and spirits. William Clarke, the force behind the All-England XI, earned his place in cricket history partially due to his marrying the landlady of the Trent Bridge Inn in Nottingham and opening a cricket ground there.[14]

These were merely the most prominent of the sport's early landmarks of the game which could be linked to the drinks trade. The commercial opportunities inherent in the ability of a cricket match to draw large crowds together for considerable lengths of time was not lost on the purveyors of alcohol. As early as 1668, London publicans were paying local property tax rates for cricket fields and the sale of beer at 'kricketing' was being licensed by Maidstone magistrates.[15] By the late eighteenth century, the commercial possibilities of cricket were being exploited evermore creatively by publicans – London pubs staged matches that pitted teams of one-armed and one-legged players against each other, one man and a dog versus two gentlemen, and a team of married women facing a team of 'maidens'.[16] As the game grew in popularity in the 1830s and 1840s and its commercial rewards increased, it became increasingly common for ex-professionals who had finished their careers to become pub landlords themselves. Yet, as we have seen with prizefighters, and numerous other sportsmen over the following century, success in sport was not an automatic gateway to success in the drinks trade, as many ex-cricketers – among them J.T. Brown, Tom Emmett, William Lockwood and Bobby Peel – became alcoholic or bankrupt ex-publicans.

The Pub and the Rise of Modern Sport

The advent of an urban industrial society heralded the beginnings of a change in the role of the pub. The exigencies of industrial work and time discipline saw the erosion of many traditional practices based on the pub. The centrality of feasts and fairs to the patterns and organisation of recreation was undermined and Saint Monday, in most towns and cities, disappeared under pressure from employers seeking greater work discipline. Drunkenness not only became a widespread social evil but it also came to be perceived as such: the passing of the Beer Act of 1830, whereby any ratepayer could obtain a two-guinea licence to sell beer, was introduced to undermine the popularity of the gin palaces, and had the effect of diluting the power of the landlord. The influence of the church and growing moral revulsion towards cruelty to animals, at least as practised in working-class pubs, saw cockfighting outlawed by Parliament in 1849, removing a regular feature of many pubs' entertainment. The rise of the temperance movement forced the drinks industry onto the back foot, more so as the moral crusade of reformers also encompassed opposition to sports they saw as crude or lewd. By banning gambling in pubs, the Betting Houses Act of 1853 removed another major attraction of the pub, although it remained a centre for illegal betting until the 1960s. The opening of public parks and other civic amenities from the 1830s also provided new outlets for recreation – indeed, the drinks trade opposed many moves to provide such facilities on the rates, rightly seeing them as a threat to their dominance of the leisure market. And, as Brian Harrison has noted, the railway dealt the greatest blow to the drink seller: by 1850 stage-coaching was all but dead, taking with it not only drinking places along the coaching routes but also much of the raison d'etre of the big city pubs.[17]

Paradoxically, the commercial success of the entrepreneurial landlord was also helping to undermine the centrality of the pub to sport and recreation. From the 1830s the popularity of music in pubs had seen the gradual development of singing or music saloons. Often the only form of organised entertainment available in working-class communities, by the 1840s the saloons had become major businesses in themselves and had begun their transformation into music halls. The boom in music hall reached its peak in 1870 when there were 415 large halls in Britain, along with countless smaller establishments.[18] Similarly the promotion of sports involving human physical activity, such as foot-racing, bowls and cricket, also laid the basis for alternative routes for the pursuit of leisure outside the pub. From being the conduit through which almost all popular sport was organised, the pub was becoming one of a number of recreational options available to the population at large, a population which from the 1870s had begun to experience a rise in its standards of living and levels of disposable income.

This contradictory relationship with the growth of mass spectator sport in the last third of the century was highlighted by the rise of football. Both the association and rugby codes of football sprang from the public schools and worked their way downwards, finding a deep resonance among the working class. Unlike virtually every other sport, they had no prior connection with the pub or the drinks trade in general. As clubs were set up and large crowds assembled to watch matches, publicans responded through their traditional role as entrepreneurs, most obviously by the renting out of grounds and changing rooms. How much of an impetus publicans actually provided to the initial formation and growth of clubs is however open to doubt – there were few other places in towns or villages that would be able to let out rooms in which a football team could change or hold meetings and, other than public parks, few institutions which also had grounds on which the game could be played.

The relationship to the sport differed fundamentally from that which pubs enjoyed with the 'traditional' sports of the first half of the century and, in many parts of the country, continued to enjoy with sports such as coursing or quoits. Whereas these sports were commercially organised by pubs and survived in large measure due to the patronage of the landlord, football was not beholden in the same way, having its origins and existence independent of the drinks trade. This could be seen in the frequency with which clubs moved grounds in order to secure better facilities and more advantageous terms. Sunderland, for example, played their first matches on a field next to the Blue House Inn but found the £10 annual rent too much so moved to a site at Ashbrooke. Everton, despite being deeply indebted to the brewer John Houlding and playing in the field adjoining his Sandon Hotel, quarrelled with him over rental charges, which led to him founding Liverpool FC. Hunslet rugby club was forced to move when the landlord of the Cemetery Tavern, emboldened by the rapid success of the side, raised the rent for the use of his pitch to £365 per year. Spurs' decision to move to play on a field attached to the White Hart Inn was made for strictly economic reasons.[19]

Conversely, some landlords found that it was to their advantage to have a football club attached to their pub: after falling out with Woodhouse rugby club in Leeds in 1893, the publican, Mark Higgins sued the team for the return of money and goods he had loaned them over the previous two years to help with 'incentives' paid to players, at the time illegal under rugby union rules, which included two gallons of free beer at every match.[20] Nevertheless, many clubs did develop long and mutually beneficial relationships with the pubs that provided them with facilities. Many junior football sides took their names from their local pub and other sides took their nicknames from the pubs in which they changed; for this reason Swinton rugby club was named the Lions and their near neighbours Broughton Rangers were less obviously known as Mrs Boardman's Boys following the name of the landlady of their headquarters. Pontypridd RFC was similarly known as the Butcher's Arms Boys in its formative years. Reversing the usual trend, when the landlord of the pub which Kilmarnock used for changing rooms decided to move in 1883, the club went with him.[21]

An analysis of shareholdings in football clubs before 1915 demonstrates that, although publicans played an important role in the financing and administration of both association and rugby clubs in this period, they were not the dominant force they had once been in sport. Using the occupational categories of the 1911 Census, 14.9 per cent of shareholders in association clubs were proprietors and employers associated with the drink trade, and they held 6.9 per cent of the total shares available. The figures were similar for the professional rugby clubs of the Northern Union: 13.1 per cent of the shareholders in rugby clubs were from the same occupational category and they owned 15.2 per cent of the shares issued. In Scottish soccer, the involvement of the drinks trade was even higher: 11.3 per cent of shareholders were proprietors or employees in the trade who owned 31.2 per cent of all shares issued. A look at the number of club directors who were involved in the trade in 1914 demonstrates the same pattern: 14.7 per cent of directors of English First Division clubs were from the trade, as were 10.1 per cent of Second Division clubs. Northern Union rugby clubs mirrored this percentage with the drinks trade making up 14.5 per cent of all directors. Again, in Scotland the figures were somewhat higher, with 21.8 per cent of First Division and 15.8 per cent of Second Division directors being from the trade.[22] Other than in the percentage of shares held in Scottish soccer clubs, representatives of the drinks trade were not first in any category.

Rather than football being an adjunct of the pub, the pub almost became an adjunct of football. Regular updates of games in progress and results of matches were sent by telegraph to pubs on Saturday afternoons, pubs put the trophies won by local teams on display, and savings clubs were set up in pubs so that their patrons could save for important away matches. In 1895 the Scarborough Hotel in the centre of Leeds advertised that it could provide match updates every ten minutes during big games. The pub became a key outlet for the sale of Saturday night football specials – such was the importance of these newspapers that in 1908 Birmingham brewery Mitchells and Butlers held two boardroom discussions on which paper to supply to their chain of pubs.[23]

For players, the provision of a pub tenancy became an especially attractive inducement to change clubs, even more so for those players playing in a nominally amateur competition, such as Scottish soccer before 1893 or northern rugby prior to the 1895 split, where it could easily be used to disguise payments for play. Scots players were often enticed to English clubs by the opportunity to run or work in a pub and the number of rugby players in Lancashire and Yorkshire who happened to be pub landlords became something of standing joke – of the thirty-five players who played for the Yorkshire rugby union side in the 1892/3 season, ten were publicans. Celtic were also well known for the number of footballing publicans in their side in the 1890s. Tony Mason has identified six Blackburn Rovers players of the early 1880s as being publicans while they were playing for the club and notes that in the 1890s it was rumoured that up to half the Sunderland side were publicans.[24] For those without the inclination or the skills to run a pub, jobs as pub waiters were available, again as a means of circumventing payment restrictions and of providing employment which did not interfere with football. Indeed, it was such a common way of avoiding payment regulations that the occupation was specifically outlawed when the Northern Union rugby authorities drew up that sport's professional regulations in 1898.

Although the presence of footballers serving in or running a pub seemed to hark back to the earlier days of boxers running pubs, in fact it was more indicative of the shift which had taken place in the relationship between sport and the pub. Footballers were given jobs in pubs by breweries in order to attract custom; the drinks trade was in fact capitalising on the popularity of the sport, rather than vice versa. Following the flotation of Guinness in 1886, the next fourteen years saw a rush to market which saw 260 breweries float on the stock market. The immense sums of capital raised in this way were used to finance the purchase of pubs to turn them into 'tied' houses, whereby they only sold beers and beverages made by, or at least approved by, their owning brewery, thus securing distribution channels against their competitors. Although this was not a new phenomenon, particularly in London, the rate at which it was carried out was. By 1890, around 70 per cent of all pubs were tied. Competition increased dramatically and so did the ways in which pubs sought to bring in customers; temperance campaigners were especially disturbed at 'devious devices such as "high kickers" and "female pianists" [which] were employed to attract custom'.[25]

Footballers were one more such 'devious device'. The widespread suspicions of the temperance reformers that pubs employing such sales tactics tended to be more prone to financial difficulties seemed to have some basis in fact. Bankruptcy, alcoholism or a combination of both often conspired against the footballing publican, most notably for former England rugby captain Dicky Lockwood, who, despite having been one of the most famous men in the north of England, could not escape bankruptcy proceedings in 1897 as he was forced to leave The Queen at Heckmondwike. Nor was a site next to a football ground an automatic passport to commercial success. Despite a huge invest-ment of £35,000 in the White Hart Inn at Tottenham, Whitbread struggled for many years to make it a success and the Cardigan Arms in Leeds almost closed in 1890 despite being directly opposite Cardigan Fields, home to St John's, the leading rugby club in Leeds, and host to international and county matches.[26] As was the case for boxers and cricketers in earlier times, success in the job could never be taken for granted by sporting publicans, nor, for that matter, for publicans in general, and it is probable that the rate of failure among sportsmen was little different to that of the population as a whole.

Nevertheless, breweries usually viewed proximity to a football ground as an important asset for a pub. The directors of Mitchells and Butlers were informed in 1910 that their pubs within the vicinity of the Hawthorns, West Bromwich Albion's ground, showed increased takings on the Saturdays of home matches. Whitbread decided that it was worth surrendering the licence of another pub in order to open a refurbished White Hart Inn and Brickwood's, the Portsmouth brewers, agreed to local magistrates' demands that they close four beer houses before they were given permission to open a new pub, The Pompey, next to Portsmouth FC's ground.[27]

The shift in the locus of popular sport away from the pub to the football ground from the 1880s was widely noticed. As early as 1883 a Blackburn publican had complained that, apart from a few pubs, by emptying the bars on a Saturday afternoon, football had been bad for business; Routledge's *Handbook of Football* noted that the popularity of football meant that 'the public houses were emptied of their thoughtless occupants, and all the vicious amusements were abandoned,' and James Miller, who first led and then opposed the move to introduce 'broken-time' payments into rugby, disparagingly commented that northern football spectators were 'the same crowd which formerly followed rabbit-coursing, dog-fighting and matters of that description'.[28] The pub's declining influence over the new mass sports was also reflected in the importance of temperance reformers to the growth of soccer, especially men like William MacGregor, Charles Sutcliffe and John Lewis who were the driving force behind the formation of the Football League in 1888.

The rise of football was one of a series of changes in the second half the nineteenth century which had a profound impact on the recreational role of the pub. Its decline in importance as a social and commercial centre was underlined by the economic difficulties faced by the drinks trade throughout this period. After reaching a peak in 1874, the demand for beer fell steeply – by 1886 demand had plummeted by 20 per cent. Between 1880 and 1890 the trade found itself in a trough as demand failed to pick up. A.E. Dingle has pointed out that as working-class wage levels rose, the demand for beer was relatively inelastic and the extra income was spent on more and better food.[29] The popularity of tobacco also started to rise rapidly during the last two decades of the century, competing with drink for working-class disposal income. The flotation mania of the 1880s and the consequent extension of the tied house system was an attempt to solve the problem of falling demand and over-capacity. The increased interest in commercial sport from the trade was part of this response. Nor was it the only response: music, the other pillar of pub entertainment, received new attention from the trade in the 1880s – the *Leicester Town Crier* noted in 1882 that pub music had re-emerged as 'one of the methods which is being largely adopted to bolster up the fall off in the liquor trade'.[30]

The consolidation of the brewing industry and the tying of the vast majority of pubs in England and Wales to brewers which took place from 1885 greatly intensified competition between pubs. By 1900 approximately 90 per cent of all pubs in England and Wales were tied. The tie meant that the nature of the pub was changing too, as they were transformed increasingly into retail units of the parent brewery, quantitatively accelerating a process which had emerged in London as far back as the 1830s.[31] This was highlighted by the steep decline in the number of publicans who brewed their own beer: the proportion of beer sold nationally by publican brewers fell from 45 per cent in 1830 to just 5 per cent in 1900, and their numbers dropped from 29,381 in 1870 to 4,361 in 1900, falling to 2,284 by 1914.[32] The economic pressures on the trade in the 1900s led to a rise in pub bankruptcies, many of them as a consequence of over-optimistic predictions of the levels of return of the investments in them in the previous decade. The trade also suffered the depredations of the 1904 Licensing Act, which gave local magistrates the right to close pubs where they felt there were too many in an area. The distribution of pubs per head of the population plummeted from one for every 285 adults in 1896 to one for every 416 in 1915. Pubs faced competing pressures from within the industry too. Bottled beer, pioneered by Bass and William Younger, began to be seen as an alternative to going to the pub for an alcoholic drink and helped stimulate a move towards drinking beer at home.[33]

Most worryingly for many publicans was the rapid growth of private clubs, which provided much the same attractions as pubs, including alcohol and especially the new bottled brands, without the legal restrictions. Exploiting a legal loophole that meant private clubs were not subject to the licensing laws – which had originally been intended to benefit gentlemen's drinking clubs – the working men's, Irish and political club movement had originated in the 1870s. It underwent a huge expansion in the 1890s, growing by 85 per cent in the decade to 1896 and then doubling in membership again in the next two decades, exactly the time at which the penetration of public houses per head of the population had dropped so precipitously. Like pubs, the club movement also underwent something of a transformation in the 1890s as they began to provide better facilities and professional entertainment for their members, increasing competitive pressures on pubs.[34] Clubs with a sporting purpose – golf in particular, but also tennis, bowls, cricket and football – grew in number between 1896 and 1930 from 171 to 2,018, while their membership rose even more steeply from 36,235 to 523,802.[35] To a great extent this development represented an extension of middle-class leisure activity and the growth of segregated sporting spheres, as Mass-Observation noted in 1943: 'Today the pub is the stronghold of sport, while tennis, golf and cricket clubs are also pubs for middle-classites.'[36] But for pubs, which drew their clientele almost exclusively from the working class, the threat to their business from the new competitor was intense. Historically, the trade had always believed that 'the public house was the working man's club' and the club movement seemed to be an affront to their traditional role.[37] The newspapers of the drinks trade expended barrels of ink and acres of paper denouncing the threat to sensible drinking which the clubs represented, but little was done until the general reform of the licensing laws caused by the exigencies of the First World War. Even then it did little to reverse the shift of customers away from the pub to the club: by 1936 the proportion of pubs to clubs had decreased from just over 15 to 1 in 1905 to 4.7 to 1 in a marketplace which had seen the total number of pubs fall from just under 100,000 to just over 75,000.[38]

But this decline in the fortunes of the pub did not necessarily mean a corresponding decline in its relationship with sport. In fact, the relationship became more contradictory and complex, as elements of the traditional and modern coexisted and intermingled. The coming of football and mass spectator sport in the 1870s and 1880s is generally seen as the beginning of the 'modern' age of sport. Certainly the newly popular football codes had a different relationship to the drinks trade than 'traditional' sports and contributed to the eclipse of these sports. National governing bodies, the organisation of national league and cup structures, and a much higher level of commercial awareness were embraced by most major sports, marking a sharp break with older forms of organisation. Writing in 1885, T.H.S. Escott commented that 'one would look in vain now for the announcements of pugilistic encounters between bruisers of established and growing reputation, cock-fights, dog-fights and performances of terrier dogs . . . within the last five-and-twenty years cricket and football clubs have been formed in all the towns and most of the villages of England'.

Similarly, in the North of England the *Yorkshireman* magazine in 1884 remarked on the decline in animal and associated sports and noted that 'football has . . . emptied the "sporting grounds"'.[39] But although the overtly cruel animal sports had disappeared or been driven underground, this did not necessarily mean the extinction of other 'traditional' sports, nor in some cases, their decline. Rather, both modern and traditional sports existed side by side throughout the late Victorian and Edwardian periods, occupying different and occasionally competing spheres of leisure time. This can be most clearly seen by looking at the sports which were actively promoted by pubs in the period from 1870 to 1920.

Taking a sample of the classified advertisements placed in the *Yorkshire Post* by pubs throughout West Yorkshire between 1870 and 1920 (see table 1), we can see that many of those sports seen as belonging to a 'pre-modern' era actually retained their vitality and possibly even increased their popularity into the early decades of the twentieth century. This is most striking in the case of knur and spell, a game common in the north of England and often seen by modern commentators as an exemplar of an older sporting world.[40] As a variant of the trap ball games historically associated with pubs, the sport had a long pedigree and enjoyed great popularity across the north by the mid-nineteenth century. Many of its contests, which normally took place between individuals, were organised and promoted by publicans and often took place on pub grounds.

The All-England Knur and Spell handicap of 1870 was organised by five men, four of whom were publicans and took place in the grounds of the New Belle Vue in Wakefield. Substantial crowds gathered for matches – for example, earlier that year 2,000 people had watched a match between Messrs Taylor and Burnley at the Nelson Inn at Morley – and even for non-championship matches stakes of twenty to thirty pounds were commonplace.[41] According to the sample, the game did decline in pubs in the last two decades of the century, but rather than die or become a historical curiosity, the new century saw Knur and Spell increase its popularity as a pub sport, so much so that in 1920 it was easily the sport most commonly advertised by pubs in the region, accounting for 56 per cent of the advertised events. The strength of the sport can be gauged by the fact that in July 1920 two pubs in West Yorkshire advertised contests for £100 prize to the winner on the same weekend.

Knur and Spell was not alone in surviving into the modern age. Those sports seen as remnants of the era of cruel animal sports, shooting at birds and rabbit coursing, maintained and actually increased their popularity at precisely the point at which 'football mania' was at its height in the last two decades of the Victorian era. Shooting and coursing dominated those sports promoted by pubs in the region right up to the First World War. Both sports were important because of the opportunities afforded for gambling, something which was technically illegal inside pub premises. Coursing had long been associated with both the aristocracy and the drinks trade: the first coursing club was founded in 1776 by Lord Orford and a National Coursing Club had been established in 1858. The Waterloo Cup, the most prestigious trophy in coursing, and still today in greyhound racing, was first run for in 1836 and was named after the Liverpool pub in which Lord Sefton and his fellow

Table 1.1 *Pub Sports in West Yorkshire, 1870–1920*

| | Events advertised | | Type of sports advertised by pubs | | | | | | | | |
	Total	In pubs	Pigeon Shooting	Rabbit Coursing	Knur & Spell	Sparrow or Starling Shooting	Dog Racing	Bowls	Pedes- trianism	Darts	Misc*
1870 Jan	50	19 (38%)	7	3	4	4	1	–	–	–	–
July	36	7 (20%)	3	–	2	1	–	–	–	–	1
1880 Jan	102	54 (53%)	22	16	–	9	3	–	4	–	–
July	36	5 (14%)	3	–	–	–	–	–	2	–	–
1890 Jan	153	86 (56%)	31	37	–	12	4	–	–	1	1
July	36	3 (8%)	1	1	1	–	–	–	–	–	–
1900 Jan	142	93 (65%)	64	24	–	5	–	–	–	–	–
July	7	3 (43%)	2	–	–	–	–	1	–	–	–
1910 Jan	61	46 (75%)	21	12	5	6	1	–	–	–	1
July	25	3 (12%)	–	–	2	–	–	–	–	–	1
1920 Jan	76	31 (41%)	10	4	15	2	–	–	–	–	–
July	48	19 (39%)	–	2	13	–	–	4	–	–	–

* Misc = Wrestling in 1870. Jumping in 1890. Shooting (at targets) in 1910.
Source: Classified advertisements in the *Yorkshire Post*, 1870–1920

coursing enthusiasts met. But the weight of accusations of cheating and sharp practice, together with its unvarnished association with gambling, had by the end of the century dramatically reduced the involvement of the upper classes in the sport. Revulsion among the middle classes towards animal cruelty probably also played its part, as more often than not the rabbit which was chased by the racing dogs was caught and killed. Although meetings were still occasionally held on the estates of the landed gentry, the focus for the sport increasingly became the pub, and it would appear that the sport's survival from the end of the century until the 1920s – when it was effectively superseded by greyhound racing, its modernist descendent – was almost entirely due to the patronage of the pub landlord.

As with coursing, shooting was especially suited to betting – even more so, as it allowed spectators to gamble throughout a contest, increasing the entertainment as the odds see-sawed according to the fortunes of the shooters. An 1870 report of a pigeon-shooting match at the Craven Heifer in Denholme noted that: 'betting was very heavy, opening at 5–4 on Kaye, but as the match proceeded, the odds rose to 3–1 against Woodhead, the latter of whom lost by one bird'.[12] The publican, who was often the bookmaker, did not rely solely on the thirst of attendant spectators to boost his income. Not only did spectators have to pay an entrance fee but so did participants, often as high as seven shillings and sixpence for bigger contests. In 1900 the Angel at Allerton Bywater near Castleford advertised a shooting competition for the prize of a pig, the privilege of shooting for which would cost shooters ten shillings; even those watching would be charged sixpence for entrance and a further shilling and sixpence for refreshments after the shoot.

Pubs had begun to promote pigeon-shooting contests in Northumberland in 1872 but they had already become commonplace in Yorkshire pubs by 1870. In Scotland too, the sport was being regularly organised by 1870. Our sample of classified advertising of sports events appearing in the *Yorkshire Post* shows that pigeon-, sparrow- and starling-shooting contests were the most frequent commercial sporting activity organised in pubs between 1870 and 1910, reaching a high point in 1900 when shooting comprised almost 74 per cent of the sports advertised. All of these contests were for money, with prizes ranging from £5 to £100 for the contests between top shooters. There were also occasionally non-monetary prizes, such as the 'fat pig' offered by both the Railway Hotel at Church Fenton and the Angel Inn near Castleford. The landlord was usually the stakeholder and referee, and on occasions a contestant; for example John Truman, the landlord of the Durham Ox Inn in Ilkeston in Derbyshire attempted to shoot fifty pigeons out of 100 for a stake of £100.[43]

Guns were remarkably easy to acquire at this time – in 1910 the *Licensed Trade News* was carrying advertisements for shotguns, rifles and revolvers at prices ranging from five shillings and sixpence to three pounds and fifteen shillings. There was surprisingly little concern about possible proliferation of firearms and in 1908 the Army Council decided that rifle ranges on licensed premises could be officially recognised as long as they had separate entrances and no alcohol was sold on a ground which was used for shooting. Pigeons and sparrows and occasionally starlings were the most favoured targets, although 'claybirds' began to be used in gentlemen's gun clubs and shooting schools from the 1890s and there was a vogue for shooting at glass balls, the precursors of the clay pigeon, in Scotland around the same time. For the specialist pigeon shooter, guns with bigger chambers were specially designed to hold more shot and powder than a normal shotgun.[44]

It appears that as pigeon shooting became identified with pubs it declined in popularity among middle-class shooters, marked by the Prince of Wales's decision to stop attending pigeon-shooting contests at Hurlingham, allegedly because his wife objected to the huge number of pigeons killed. The association of the sport with gambling also undermined its appeal to the middle classes: 'it is very trying on the nerves, even of men not ordinarily nervous, to shoot in the presence of a crowd round the firing point, many of them bookmakers, whose business it is to express criticism of the shooting in the form of odds for or against the bird's escape,' wrote *Licensing World* sympathetically in 1900.[45] In contrast, it was precisely this which made the sport so appealing to shooters and spectators from lower down the social order. There is evidence that there was some mixing of the classes in pub shooting contests in the 1870s – for example, the Bank House Inn at Pudsey near Leeds hosted a match for £5 between J. Bywater and an anonymous amateur in 1870 – but as with the football codes, this mixing of classes for leisure was to be short-lived. However, it was not until the 1920 Firearms Control Act, which severely restricted the availability and use of guns in the wake of worries about the spread of revolution from Russia and civil war in Ireland, that shooting disappeared as a pub sport.[46]

Scotland presents a very different picture of the relationship between sport and the pub. From the available evidence, it appears that the pub, whilst important to sport, did not play such a central role in its organisation or in the survival of older sports during this period. A survey of classified advertisements in the *Glasgow Herald* for the 1870-1920 period revealed no advertisements whatsoever from pubs advertising sports events. We have been able to locate only two reports of pubs being involved in the organising of sports events, as opposed to hosting after-match entertainments or meetings of clubs or associations: the Old Oak Inn at Denny hosted a quoits handicap in July 1880 and the Clydesdale Harriers began a race from the Moss Side Inn at Paisley in 1890. A search of the *Glasgow Evening Times* for the same period was similarly barren. Of course, this is not to say that pubs in the Glasgow area were uninvolved in sports at this time – we have already noted their importance for committee meetings, refreshment and changing facilities, especially for soccer – but it does suggest that their importance to the organisation of what were seen in the south as 'pub sports', such as quoiting, bowls and shooting, was substantially less significant than in England.

This view is reinforced by the number of reports from quoiting, bowling and curling clubs throughout Scotland which had their own grounds, apparently unconnected with pubs. When William Drysdale of Dalkeith beat Alva's Andrew Hunter for the quoits 'world championship at 18 yards' and £50 in 1890, he did it at the Grangeham Quoiting Ground at Bo'ness, unlike Messrs Jackson and Howson who met to decide the Knur and Spell 'championship and £100' at the New Queens Inn at Barnsley in 1870.[47] Compared to England, Scottish sport was far more organised and self-sustaining. By the latter quarter of the century, many sports there had developed national and local associations and competitions and were not dependent on the largesse or entrepreneurial spirit of a publican for their organisation. The commonly accepted rules of bowls had been drawn up in 1848 in Glasgow and local bowling associations had existed at least two decades before the formation of the Scottish Bowling Association in 1892 – in 1870 Kilmarnock clubs took part in the annual Silver Bowl competition and twenty clubs contested the Glasgow Bowling Association Cup in the same year. In contrast, the English Bowling Association was founded in 1903 and even the local associations of the popular Northern English crown green bowling game did not begin to be formed until the late 1880s. Even more notably, the Grand Caledonian Curling Club had been formed in 1838 and in 1880, by which time it had received royal patronage and replaced 'Grand' with 'Royal', it had 409 member clubs, plus another 114 outside of Scotland. Quoiting too had a national competition and local leagues in place by at least 1900.[48] In many ways, it could be argued that these high levels of organisation and national structures from the mid-nineteenth century onwards suggest that 'modernity' came earlier to Scottish sports than to those in England.

The one exception to this was angling, which was closely connected with the hotel and the pub. This appears to have been the case both for the aristocratic and the artisan fisherman. In July 1890, of 167 angling events reported in the *Glasgow Herald*, sixty-two, or 37 per cent, were organised from or took place at inns or hotels. One took place at the Langholm distillery and another was organised from the Temperance Hotel in Strathyre. Many of the hostelries involved were sited on lochs or rivers, which was obviously a major source of their appeal. A significant number of these reports were concerned with the catches of only one or two anglers and many took place during the week, suggesting a high degree of upper- and middle-class involvement, particularly at holiday times.

But if the Scottish pub did not play such a critical role in the organisation of sport as its English counterpart, it would be a mistake to draw the conclusion that it had no importance in the organisation of Scottish sport. Many pubs across Scotland provided grounds for various sports and many publicans offered trophies or cash prizes for local competitions. Even when a sport was organised independently of the drinks trade and had its own structure, publicans often played an important role: in 1901 the medals for the Stirling and District Quoiting Association championship were provided by Robert Morgan, landlord of Stirling's Douglas Hotel, who was also president of the association that year. And despite many clubs having their own grounds, in certain localities the pub was vital to the continuation of various sports; for example, Milngavie West End Bowling Club, noted for its working-class membership, was heavily dependent on the support of the landlord of the local Douglas Arms throughout the 1890s, both for the improvement of the green and for his refusal to sell it during the 'building boom' at the turn of the century. The town's quoiting clubs also used grounds attached to the Douglas Arms and the Black Bull Inn.[49]

Quoits in particular had close associations with the pub on both sides of the border. At least as early as 1830 teams representing Falkirk and Stirling had played each other on grounds owned by pubs and the popularity of the game, and the rewards available to its successful practitioners, can be gauged by the fact that in 1850 John Rennie of Alva and a Mr Heywood of Oldham played a match for a stake of £100 in a pub near Newcastle railway station. The following year it was reported that an Edinburgh publican had made £300 in bets from the 600 spectators who saw Rennie take on Pollockshaw's Mr Ewing at Bruntsfield Links in the city. In 1875 the Abbey Arms at Plaistow played host to another £100 match between Glasgow's D. Haddow and London's George Graham.[50] In England, the sport was generally viewed as a working-class sport, not without reason, as it was especially popular among miners in the North-East, Somerset and Kent. In the 1880s, fifty-two pubs in thirty-three villages in Northumberland had quoits grounds, a number of which had seating installed for spectators.[51] Perhaps because of this, quoits in England gained a reputation for attracting violent spectators, especially when contrasted with bowls. Giving evidence to the 1929 Royal Commission, Superintendent Ernest Stewart of the Carlisle Constabulary declared:

We used to say up north, if you want to be a good quoiter, you have to be a good fighter. People are not encouraged to come to a special bowling match, but you will see in a public house window 'The Hand Inn will hold their annual quoit match on Saturday', and that is advertised through the country[sic], and at the quoit match you get a certain undesirable class that a policeman does not like . . . Fighting and quoiting go together generally.[52]

How accurate an assessment of the sport this was must be slightly open to doubt, especially as W. Bently Capper's 1923 guide to running a pub recommended bowling, angling and quoits as three of the most popular sports that a pub could promote. Certainly in Scotland the game did not carry the same associations of unruliness and had been seen as a rival to the attractions of 'the dram shop'. But despite Capper's recommendation, the sport was in serious decline in the inter-war period: the last world championship was staged in 1913 and despite attempts to organise international matches between England, Scotland and Wales, it appears that Mass-Observation's view that in Bolton the game was dying out and being replaced by darts, was also true for the game in Britain as a whole.[53]

Pub Sports and Sporting Culture

Across Britain, the pub was more than simply an organising point for sport or a source of facilities. Sport itself was an integral part of the day-to-day culture of the pub, regardless of any active involvement its patrons may have, and was inevitably a major topic of conversation: in the mid-1880s James Burnley noted that the patrons of pubs he visited in the Bradford area spent their time discussing dogs, coursing, pigeon-flying and gambling on pedestrianism. Fifty years later, Mass-Observation calculated that 29 per cent of the conversations their investigators overheard in Bolton pubs were about sport, and recorded an even higher figure of 37 per cent for London pubs. In St Helens in Lancashire in the 1920s, the importance of sport to the daily conversations of one pub was attested to by the presence of a miner's diary kept behind the bar. This recorded, among other things, detailed sporting records of the area and was regularly used to settle disputes among customers. A Mass-Observation investigator in Birmingham noted in June 1947 that 'there is solid evidence in pubs that football is the main topic when in season. A number of the pubs have photographic records of the club and even now there is still football talk.' The following year the same investigator recorded the comment of a drinker in an Aston pub: 'Football and beer, that's the only two things you'll find up here.' In parts of Cumbria and Snowdonia, certain pubs became closely identified with the culture of rock climbing and, as perhaps could be expected, were divided between those frequented by working-class climbers and those patronised by those of the middle classes. The pleasures of a sporting discussion over a drink did not go unnoticed by advertisers either. The 1938 spring annual of *The Cricketer* carried an advertisement for Black & White whisky in which an imaginary 'average man' spoke about the enjoyment of 'arguing the merits of my team just too much with the plumber sitting on my left as with the retired Colonel on the other side. And as likely as not we'll all three adjourn to pick the next Test side over a "Black & White".'[54]

Such discussions were an indispensable constituent of the conversational glue which held together the 'masculine republic' of the pub. Both the pub and sport were almost exclusively the domain of the male, places where men would usually go to enjoy the company of other men and avoid the presence of women – Mass-Observation found that in Bolton in the late 1930s no more than 25 per cent of the customers in pubs were women, even at the weekends when it could be expected that socialising between the sexes would bring more women into pubs. The structure of the pub, were there was often a segregated area for women in the snug or lounge, was similar to that of the sports ground where separate enclosures for 'ladies' and cheaper entrance prices were common. And like the sports field, the pub was also a site of masculine ritual: fathers would get their sons drunk at a 'rearing' as part of the transition to manhood and apprentices were expected to buy drinks for their instructors as part of their admission to their chosen trade. More importantly, the act of drinking alcohol, and beer in particular, was, like participation in sport, seen as proof of masculine identity in itself. The same Mass-Observation survey reported one man who saw the consumption of beer as essential to his reputation with his friends: 'My reason for drinking is to appear tough. I heartily detest the stuff but what would my pals say if I refused. They would call me a cissy.' In a similar vein, the comedian Spike Milligan recalled the response he received at the bar of London Irish rugby union club when he decided he had drunk enough beer: 'I . . . said to the barman, "Look, I can't drink all this bloody Guinness – I'll have some wine." The bugger shouted down the bar, "A glass of wine for Mrs Milligan!"'[55] This 'masculine republic' of the pub found its highest expression in clubs, many of which combined sports facilities such as billiard or snooker tables with a blanket refusal to allow women on their premises at all.

The development of separate drinking areas for women in pubs had gathered pace in the 1890s, when breweries sought to increase the return on their investments in tied houses by making pubs more attractive and increasing their facilities. Many of the pubs opened during this period were opulent and richly designed, a far cry from the dark and dank beer houses of the mid-century, and sought to bring to themselves a level of respectability hitherto not associated with public houses. The immediate sporting beneficiary of this was billiards, which, with its aura of the gentlemen's club, helped both to increase the respectability of the pub and to offer another attraction to existing and potential patrons. The high cost of a billiards table – manufacturers' advertisements in trade journals priced them from 55 to 1,000 guineas – together with the need for a dedicated room, meant that the sport was unlikely to have found such demand without the financial clout of the breweries behind it. By the turn of the century *The Licensed Victualler* could write that 'billiards is the chief legitimate game of skill and recreation generally practised on licensed premises . . . one can scarcely imagine any properly furnished hotel or modern public house without its billiard room'.[56] The installation of a billiard room became a major selling point for a pub so equipped, helping, so it was hoped, to raise the pub above the association with drunkenness into suburban respectability; when the Thurlow Arms in West Norwood converted its stables into a billiard room and bar in 1900, one could be forgiven for assuming its description applied to the comfortable home of a member of the professional middle classes:

> There are two of Thurston's [a prominent table manufacturer] tables, which are surrounded by the most snug and ornate environment. At one end there are two French windows leading to a well-kept lawn, which will be utilised for bowls, whilst at the opposite end there is a curtained lounge and bar. There is an ample installment of electric lighting and, in fact, the apartment is as complete as human ingenuity could make it.[57]

But although the game became very popular at this time, the annual London Licensed Victuallers' championship being played for at the famous Gaiety Restaurant, its very popularity caused it to founder on the eccentricities of the licensing laws. Under Section 11 of the 1845 Gaming Act, the tables could only be played upon during licensing hours and a separate licence had to be taken out annually for billiards to be played at all. Zealous police ensured that it was not uncommon for pubs or hotels to be fined for allowing the game to be played after closing time, even if no alcohol was being served. Given these restrictions, the return on investment for the large amounts expended on billiard rooms was circumscribed to say the least, and the early years of the new century saw a move away from billiard rooms in pubs towards the opening of billiard halls and clubs in their own right. Although a licence still had to be held, tables could be used between 8 a.m. and 1 a.m., closing only on Sundays and religious holidays, offering much greater opportunities for use. By 1930, billiards in pubs was almost dead: in 1938 Mass-Observation noted that billiards was unknown in pubs and in 1929 W.T. Rainbow, the vice-president of the Billiard Table Makers Association, had told the Royal Commission on Licensing that 'the game today is played largely in public billiard rooms where only light refreshments – non-intoxicants – are supplied'.[58]

As was implied by the report on the Thurlow Arms, bowls was also a beneficiary of the increased investment in pubs and of the increased pressure on publicans to provide activities to attract customers. 'A bowling green is one of the finest attractions an inn can have,' wrote a guide to pub management in 1923, echoing a widespread belief in the trade.[59] The sport had one of the oldest associations with the pub, dating back to at least the thirteenth century, and whether played in one of its many indoor or outdoor varieties was always seen as being among the most English of games, not least because of its association with Sir Francis Drake, who allegedly decided to continue with his game at the Pelican Arms in Plymouth despite being told of the approach of the Spanish Armada in July 1588. It was popular also because it was easy to organise and indoor bowling or skittle alleys were common during the Elizabethan period. Indeed, it was more often than not the pub which brought the sport to a particular locality; for example, the first bowling green in Gloucester was opened in 1604 at the New Inn. The identification of pubs with their greens led to many adopting the name Bowling Green Inn or some variant of it. 'From time immemorial,' rhapsodised the *Licensed Victualler*, bowls had been linked 'with the village inn and many of the innkeepers [who held] championships in their respective districts'.[60]

But by 1801 Joseph Strutt could claim in his *The Sports and Pastimes of the People of England* that the game was dying out and, although Strutt tended to exaggerate the decline of traditional sports, it does appear to have decreased in popularity during the first half of the nineteenth century. The high premium on urban land in the early part of the 1800s led to many pubs selling their bowling greens: by 1848 Birmingham had only one bowling green left in the city centre and even this was sold off during that year. However, as Alan Metcalfe has noted, bowls was especially popular among Durham and Northumberland miners in mid-century and there was a succession of recognised coalfield champions between the 1830s and 1850s. In Scotland too the game continued to be popular, with many pubs providing bowling greens and landlords offering trophies and prize money. In 1858 the Westerton Arms at Bridge of Allan hosted a tournament of 150 bowlers from all over Scotland to compete for a silver claret jug, the first time, it was believed, that such a nationwide contest had ever been held.[61] As leisure time and purchasing power increased from the 1870s the sport had begun to enjoy a fresh lease of life, most notably in the north of England and Scotland, where, by 1900, the Scottish Bowling Association, which had been founded in 1892, had 229 clubs, most of which were unconnected with pubs. In contrast, the preservation and revival of the game in the north of England had almost entirely been due to the licensed trade: innkeeper Henry Wardle sponsored Newcastle's first annual bowling handicap in 1867 and the extent of the game's popularity in Lancashire can be gauged from the fact that in 1902 a Mr Sloan undertook a walking tour of all pub bowling greens in the county, covering 2,000 miles despite finishing his journey at Eccles, a town barely 10 miles from his starting point in Bolton.[62]

In the south of England it was a different matter, and commentators at the turn of the century noted both the decline of the sport itself and its links with the pub. In some areas it retained its popularity, such as Southampton, which claimed to have had a bowling club dating back to 1299 and where the Knighthood competition had been run continuously since 1776, but such was its decline in the capital that in 1900 the London County Council decided to open bowling greens on municipal parks, as it was almost impossible to find a bowling club in the metropolis. The sport was also helped by the growth in the number of bowling clubs with their own licensed premises. In many ways, the new clubs helped to supply the sporting facilities which pubs had previously done. Between 1896 and 1930 the number of licensed bowling clubs rose from eighty-three to 465 and membership increased fivefold to over 56,000.[63]

Nevertheless, in the north and midlands of England, by far the majority of bowling greens continued to be provided by pubs. In 1938 Mass-Observation noted that most bowls played in Bolton was played on pub greens and by 1950 Mitchells and Butlers still had over 150 pubs with their own bowling greens in the Birmingham area alone.[64] In Bolton, as in Birmingham and much of Lancashire and Yorkshire, pub bowls was played on crown greens, whereby the centre of the green was raised to make the aiming of the bowls more difficult, whereas flat greens were used by church teams, and were more common in the south of England. Bowls was also noticeable for being a sport in which working-class women, often middle-aged and older, took part regularly, although the absence of statistical evidence makes their involvement impossible to quantify. As early as 1878, members of the Allander Bowling Club in Scotland competed for the 'Landlady's Prize' donated by Mrs McMurtrie of the Black Bull Hotel, although it is not known if women took part in the competition.[65] Certainly by 1902 women were playing on an organised basis in Lancashire and the Midlands, and in 1906 London County Council laid aside one green for women bowlers in each park. The importance that pub bowling competitions had in their local communities was highlighted by Mass-Observation who noted that it was a way in which the culture of the pub linked up with the 'official' life of the town. Bolton's Infirmary Cup was played to raise funds for the local hospital and was attended by local dignitaries; this relationship continued in places even up into the 1970s; in Norfolk, for example, the president of the county bowls association was a member of the Steward & Patterson Brewery family. In this, bowls appears in some ways to have partially recreated the inclusive, cross-class leisure patterns of pre-industrial times, when the sport of the common people took place under the patronage of the gentry. Indeed, much of the appeal of bowls was based on its associated imagery of summer, green fields and leisurely playing time so redolent of English pastoralism – and for many working-class players and spectators, the bowling green may well have been the only green field within walking distance. A similar appeal, albeit a more exclusively masculine one, was engendered by angling, a sport which also made extensive use of pub facilities and whose competitions had been promoted by pub landlords since at least the 1850s.[66]

As Brian Harrison has noted, 'the urban pub has always, even in its architectural styles, embodied the urban Englishman's desire to flee into the country . . . the traditions, the ceremonial, the sociability, and even the sports of rural life were all preserved by urban publicans'.[67] This sense that the pub helped to continue the traditions of the rural past, including those of animal cruelty, was also invoked by many other aspects of pub sporting life, even its decoration. Sporting prints had long been a feature of the decor of all but the meanest drinking house. Like pub signs themselves, they often sought to reflect the local sporting culture, albeit in an idealised and romantic way, providing a link to earlier, more rural times. In 1908 J. Fairfax Blakeborough commented:

> over the country one found the prevailing sport illustrated on the walls of the licensed houses in each locality. Go where you will amongst Durham pit villages and you find pictures of famous greyhounds and coursing men of note; travel over the borders into Northumberland, and you begin to find salmon fishing and angling generally represented; . . . So it is everywhere that the hostel catches the sporting infection.[68]

The popularity of sporting prints took on a new lease of life with the advent of modern advertising and marketing techniques in 1880s and 1890s. Sport became a well-mined seam for advertisements, posters and beer mats. This became particularly true with the advent of bottled beers, as brewers sought to tempt publicans to stock their brands by offering pictures and prints as inducements. Distillers and manufacturers of the newly fashionable sparkling waters also used the same marketing techniques. The huge investments in pubs of the 1890s and early 1900s, and the efforts of the brewers to make their newly-tied pubs more attractive and congenial, also contributed to the sporting print's new lease of life, allowing suppliers of sporting illustrations, such as Birmingham's Henry Graves & Co, to make a healthy living.

The increasing use of such devices to increase the attractiveness of pubs was one more manifestation of the trade's realisation that it had to exploit every opportunity to attract and retain customers. Numerous articles were published offering advice to publicans about how to make their establishments more appealing: the *Licensed Victuallers' Gazette* published a series of articles at the end of the century the aim of which was 'to lay before our readers information upon the lawful games that may be played by persons visiting licensed houses'. The series endorsed thirty-three sports and games, ranging through sports as diverse as shove-halfpenny and wrestling. For those wondering what lay beyond the law, it specified 'Ace of Hearts. Baccarat, Basset, Dice, Faro, Hazard, Passage. And any game or games played for money or money's worth (though otherwise permissible).'[69] But the associations with gambling were impossible to shake off, not least because it was one of the appeals of pub life. As we have seen, the popularity of many pub sports was based to a great extent on the opportunities for gambling which they afforded. Just as football results were telegraphed to pubs, so too were the results of horse races. The availability of sporting newspapers in pubs made them places where form could be studied and discussed. Virtually every pub had at least one bookmaker's agent, or runner, among its clientele and the threat of intervention by the police against illegal gambling activities was an occupational hazard for most pubs. Those that didn't offer the facility, especially in urban areas, ran the risk of losing a significant number of customers. Indeed, Canon Peter Green of Salford claimed in the 1920s that only six publicans in his area did not allow betting and that one of them had found business so bad because of this that he left the trade.[70]

Like Bently Capper's mammoth three-volume guide to pub management published in the early 1920s and a range of other similar publications published in the first decades of the twentieth century, the *Gazette's* series also sought to instill a greater commercial awareness in the publican and alert him to the economic opportunities inherent in pub sports. The underlying implication was that, unlike older times when the public had few alternatives but to visit the pub for their leisure, now the publican had to compete for business and that sport was a powerful magnet for customers. As Capper pointed out:

> therein lies the golden rule for achieving popularity – the popularity that pays in bigger profits: interest yourself in those sports and pastimes in which your customers are interested . . . Encourage the formation of clubs which will naturally make your house their headquarters; and if, as in the case of a cricket or football club, you cannot provide the ground,

you can still place a room at the team's disposal for changing in, and encourage the holding of the committee meetings at your house.[71]

This 'golden rule' assumed an even greater importance in the inter-war years as the trade continued to face difficulties. Expenditure on drink fell by a third, beer consumption fell similarly, the number of pubs declined by 10 per cent between 1919 and 1936, while breweries in the same period saw their ranks reduced from 3,000 to 1,100. These problems were due to a combination of three factors: the continuation of the structural difficulties of the pre-war period, increased competition from other leisure activities, and restrictive legal changes. New rivals such as the cinema, the radio, local libraries and gardening allotments, which under the impact of the war had increased tenfold, all helped to undermine the pub's dominance of leisure time. Old rivals such as the club movement, which continued to grow rapidly, and the off-licence, which capitalised on the growing popularity of drinking bottled beer at home, sales of which accounted for 30 per cent of all beer sold by 1939, further eroded the pub's influence. Governmental policy played a role too, as wartime restrictions on opening hours, originally imposed in 1915 as a means of increasing production, and higher duties on beer, which rose from seven shillings and ninepence per barrel to a hundred shillings, were continued, making draught beer both more difficult and more expensive to buy.

And beer now had a serious competitor for the disposable income of the working classes: tobacco, expenditure on which increased fivefold between 1914 and 1939 while per capita consumption almost doubled. Tobacco also laid claim to the same associations with sport that the pub had traditionally thought of as its own. Cigarette cards featuring famous teams and players of every popular sport, but especially football, captured the imaginations of generations of young boys and men, and the advertising of the product sought to establish its health-giving properties in much the same way as beer had always done. By 1948, 80 per cent of all men and 41 per cent of women were smokers, thereby reducing the disposable income available for alcohol.

Nevertheless, in the face of such problems publicans retained the historic resilience of their trade and adapted to the changing times. Throughout Britain, the pub still retained its importance as a provider of facilities to sports of varying kinds: Bessie Reed, whose seventy years in the trade started before the First World War, recalled that 'the pub clubroom was used as a changing room for local football games; a prohibition on ball games in pubs meant that until the Second World War, bagatelle, billiards and "devil amongst the tailors" had to be covered up on Sundays, Christmas and Good Fridays'.[72] Mass-Observation also noted that bowling, darts and angling clubs all had their headquarters at pubs in the Bolton area in the late 1930s. In other towns, their use as changing rooms for football and rugby teams was commonplace, in large part because, as the daughter of a St Helens licensee noted about the 1920s: 'The pub was the social centre . . . There was no TV and even darts was in its infancy.'[73] But many 'traditional' sports were lost to the pub or reduced to marginal existences. After 1920 shooting became extinct in pubs as the sight of members of the urban working class using guns became less palatable and gun licences became harder to acquire. Coursing became a victim of its modernised commercial offspring, greyhound racing. The electric hare had been developed in the United States and brought to Britain in 1925. The first track was opened at Belle Vue in Manchester and by 1927 there were sixty-two companies organising races. Such was the popularity of the sport that it was second only to soccer as Scotland's most watched sport in the 1930s.[74]

Quoits also fell into sharp decline, with many pub-based clubs and local leagues disappearing in the 1920s and 1930s, especially in the south of England, where at least Kent, Essex and Suffolk saw the game extinguished for all practical purposes.[75] Its successor as the pub sport which involved throwing objects at a target was darts, which, although there is no quantitative evidence, it is safe to assume became the most popular pub sport of all in the inter-war years. Various forms of darts had been played in pubs for centuries, but in the latter half of the nineteenth century it had acquired a reputation as a game of chance rather than skill and had been seen, especially by the police, as simply a vehicle for gambling. Dart folklore traces modern darts back to an alleged 1908 court case in which it was definitively proved to be a game of skill, although the *Licensed Victuallers' Gazette* had listed it as a recommended pub game in 1900. But the catalyst for the sport's expansion was probably the formation of the National Darts Association in 1924 by a group of publicans. The *News of the World* sponsored a London-based championship from 1927, which became a national championship in 1947. Such was the appeal of the sport that in 1939 20,000 spectators crammed into Islington's Agricultural Hall to see Marmaduke Breckton defeat Jim Pike. Despite regional variations in the rules of the game and the type of board it was played on – for example, the Yorkshire board had no treble band – the sport rapidly gained national popularity, not least because it was both easy to play for participants and simple to organise for publicans.[76] Local pub leagues were established and both team and individual competitions became a regular feature of pub life.

One particularly notable feature of pub life to which darts contributed was the participation of women in pub sport. Although men dominated at the higher levels, women's darts became possibly the most popular participation sport for women in the years following the end of the Second World War. For many women it would be one of the rare occasions on which they would visit a pub unaccompanied by a man. In 1960 a Bolton publican commented to a Mass-Observation reporter that women rarely came into his pub by themselves 'unless you count the ladies' darts team'. Women's darts was one of the most socially significant developments in pub life of the period, establishing a bridgehead into the 'masculine republic' and helping to undermine the status of the pub as an exclusively male domain. Although this was new, in many ways the darts boom helped to revivify the sense of community which had been at the heart of pub culture for centuries. The popularity of the sport drew in people from different walks of life, the organisation of the team entailed greater social contact between customers and the league structure of the sport led to a broader sense of community, often felt to be under threat as leisure activities focused more and more on the home, especially with the advent of television. The extent to which many darts clubs encouraged this sense of community was captured by a Mass-Observation reporter from a village in the south of England in 1947:

> The Darts Club has 78 members, men and women. Each member pays 6d weekly to the club. Some weeks they have a quarter week when the sub is 9d. If payments get four weeks in arrears the member is suspended.
>
> This group originally grew out of the interest which people felt in the playing of what has now become perhaps the most popular of pub games. It has now become formalised and developed a number of activities which have very little to do with playing darts but a good deal to do with the mutual aid spirit which seems to arise in any group where people get to know each other well.
>
> The Darts Club now provides for its members: 1. Darts Matches. 2. Home and Away Outings. 3. Christmas Party for the Children. 4. Party and Dinner for members. 5. Christmas Pay Out. Last year what you paid in you got paid back. Raffles covered the rest. 6. Dart Club Banking Account. 7. Derby Day Outing. Members paid 7/6, the club the rest. 8. If a member is ill over six weeks, the club gives financial assistance, has a benefits darts match etc.[77]

And for the publican, the purchase of a couple of dartboards and the provision of a few plates of sandwiches on match nights inevitably led to more drink being consumed and greater takings at the bar. It appeared to be a world where everyone was a winner.

But if the success of darts superficially suggested a revival of the role of the pub as the social centre of the community, the underlying reality was very different. The economic exigencies of the drinks industry were furthering the transformation of the pub into a simple retail outlet of a brewery. Another round of takeover, merger and consolidation took place in the 1930s – for example, between Bass and Worthington, the two giants of Burton on Trent brewing –

and again in the early 1960s, leading to increasing corporate uniformity for pubs and for beer itself. As the consumption of draught beer continued to decline into the 1960s, the local pub was tied ever more closely to brewery marketing campaigns, and the ability of the individual publican to initiate their own leisure activities for customers was severely circumscribed. Whilst many pubs continued to provide facilities for sports, especially changing rooms for football clubs, the broader social aspects of organising and promoting sports were increasingly at odds with corporate strategies to maximise pub resources.

The growth of Sunday football in the 1960s demonstrated the way in which the role of the pub had changed. The decline in observation of the Sabbath saw Sunday football gain increasing popularity during the 1960s and 1970s. Usually played in the morning, matches were commonly organised to end at the same time at which pubs opened. Many clubs used pubs as a base to meet and to change for matches and sometimes incorporated the name of their pub into their team names. No doubt the use of pubs as a base from which to undermine Sabbatarianism would have brought an ironic smile to the ghosts of those campaigners who opposed the Sunday Observance acts in the nineteenth century. However, the fact that Sunday football was largely played on municipally-owned park football pitches, rather than on fields belonging or attached to pubs, underlined the pub's declining influence over the course of the previous century. Despite the limited facilities pubs could now offer football teams, and perhaps reflecting a lack of appropriate leisure facilities elsewhere, such remained the popularity of football and the depths of its link with alcohol that pubs are still today an important base for local football, and rugby league, teams. In the latter part of the twentieth century sponsorship of football by the breweries occasionally gave a boost to the traditional link between the game and the pub by promoting inter-pub competitions, in much the same way as they had once used darts to raise their corporate profile.

Nevertheless, the overall trend since the 1960s has been one which has seen the sporting role of the pub gradually reduced, as it became a retail adjunct of brewery sponsorship or marketing projects. To a large extent, this mirrors the decline in the independence of the publican, as the commercial exigencies of the breweries, or more latterly the retail company which owns or effectively controls the pub, have exerted increasingly greater pressure to maximise profits to the exclusion of the provision of wider social facilities by the pub. By the 1980s this transformation had reached such a level that the history of the pub becomes indistinguishable from that of the breweries – the metamorphosis of the traditional pub landlord into a modern retail manager was effectively complete.

Notes

1. *The Licensed Trade News*, 31 December 1910. For the sake of brevity, we will use the term 'pub' as a short-hand term for all the varieties of drinking place, except where it is necessary to differentiate.
2. Robert Roberts, *The Classic Slum*, Manchester, 1971, p. 120.
3. Jacob Larwood and John Camden Hotten, *English Inn Signs*, Exeter, 1986, p. 47, pp. 90–7 and pp. 132–3.
4. Ibid., p. 128.
5. J. Wentworth Day, *Inns of Sport*, London, 1949, pp. 33–4.
6. Barrie Cox, *English Inn and Tavern Names*, Nottingham, 1994. List of Licences granted by Magistrates in the Halifax area to Public Houses and Beer Sellers, dated 29 August 1871, in Calderdale Archives, HA S/B: 2/13/9 and Misc:/8/116/124-136. *Aspects of Culture and Recreation in 19th Century and Early 20th Century Huddersfield*, Bretton Hall College, Urban Studies Series, no. 3, Summer 1979.
7. *Stow's Survey* of 1720, quoted in Horatio Smith, *Festivals, Games and Amusements*, London, 1831, p. 121.
8. Michael Jackson, *The English Pub*, London, 1976, p. 117.
9. Dennis Brailsford, *British Sport – A Social History*, Cambridge, 1992, p. 67.
10. Dennis Brailsford, *Bareknuckles: A Social History of Prizefighting*, Cambridge, 1988, p. 18.
11. John Ford, *Boxiana,* London, 1976 edition, pp. 185–6.
12. Vincent Dowling, *Fistiana, or Oracle of the Ring*, London, 1868, p. 143. We are indebted to Professor Peter Radford for this quote.
13. For example, *The Licensed Victualler's Mirror*, published in London, carried a long-running series 'Chronicles of the Prize Ring' from 1888 onwards. In 1900 *The Licensed Victuallers' Gazette* also published the two-volume *Fights for the Championship. The Men and their Times*, bound in half leather, costing 25 shillings.
14. Diana Raitt Kerr, *Hambledon Cricket and The Bat and Ball Inn*, Chichester, 1951. Brian Harrison, *Drink and the Victorians*, 2nd Edition, Keele, 1994, p. 49.
15. Derek Birley, *Sport and the Making of Britain*, Manchester, 1993, p. 93.
16. Neil Wigglesworth, *The Evolution of English Sport*, London, 1996, p. 26.
17. Harrison, *Drink and the Victorians*, p. 322.
18. Peter Bailey, 'Introduction: Making Sense of Music Hall' in Peter Bailey (ed.), *Music Hall, The Business of Pleasure*, Milton Keynes, 1986, p. x.
19. For football clubs, see Simon Inglis, *The Football Grounds of Great Britain*, London, Second Edition, 1987, pp. 57, 87 and 212. For Hunslet, see Tony Collins, *Rugby's Great Split*, London, 1998, pp. 33–4.
20. *Yorkshire Post*, 23 December 1893.
21. Trevor Delaney, *The Grounds of Rugby League*, Keighley, 1991, pp. 152 and 189; John Weir, *Drink, Religion and Scottish Football 1873–1900*, Renfrew, 1992, p. 22.

22. Figures taken from Wray Vamplew, *Pay Up and Play The Game*, Cambridge, 1988, pp. 156–71, and Collins, *Rugby's Great Split*, pp. 243–5. Similar findings can be found in Tony Mason, *Association Football and English Society 1863-1915*, Brighton, 1980 and Stephen Tischler, *Footballers and Businessmen*, New York, 1981.

23. *The Yorkshire Owl*, 3 April 1895. Henry Mitchell & Co. Ltd, Managing Directors Board meeting minutes, 23 and 30 April 1906.

24. Mason, *Association Football*, pp. 118–9.

25. John Chartres, 'Joshua Tetley & Son, 1890s to 1990s' in John Chartres and Katrina Honeyman (eds), *Leeds City Business*, Leeds, 1993, pp. 120–1.

26. *Yorkshire Post*, 7 January 1897; Sidney O. Neville *Seventy Rolling Years*, London, 1958, p. 177; Barrie Pepper, *Old Inns and Pubs of Leeds*, Leeds, 1997, p. 56.

27. Henry Mitchell & Co Ltd, Managing Directors Board meeting minutes, 17 January 1910; P. Eley and R.C. Riley, *The Demise of Demon Drink? Portsmouth Pubs 1900–1950*, Portsmouth 1991, p. 11. Neville, *Seventy Rolling Years*, p. 177.

28. Mason, *Association Football*, p. 175; *Routledge's Handbook of Football*, p. 10, quoted in Morris Marples, *A History of Football*, London, 1954, p. 122. James Miller quoted in *Yorkshire Post*, 18 January 1897.

29. A.E. Dingle 'Drink and Working Class Living Standards in Britain 1870–1914', *Economic History Review*, volume 25, 1972.

30. *Leicester Town Crier*, 6 January 1882, quoted in Jeremy Crump, 'Provincial Music Hall: Promoters and Public in Leicester, 1863-1929' in Bailey (ed.), *Music Hall, The Business of Pleasure,*, p. 61.

31. T.R. Gourvish and RG Wilson, 'Profitability in the Brewing Industry, 1885–1914', *Business History* vol. 27, 1985, p. 148.

32. George B. Wilson, *Alcohol and the Nation*, London, 1940, pp. 85–6.

33. See Harrison, *Drink and the Victorians*, pp. 332–7. Chartres, 'Joshua Tetley & Son, 1890s to 1990s', pp. 125–7.

34. See T.G. Ashplant , 'London Working Men's Clubs, 1875–1914' in Eileen and Stephen Yeo (eds), *Popular Culture and Class Conflict 1590–1914*, Brighton, 1981, pp. 243–58.

35. Wilson, *Alcohol and the Nation*, pp. 141–5.

36. Mass-Observation, *The Pub and the People*, London, 1943, p. 284.

37. See, for example, the speech by Henry Bentley, the President of the Yorkshire Brewer's Association in January 1880 supporting Sunday drinking. *Yorkshire Post*, 21 January 1880.

38. Statistics are taken from Wilson, *Alcohol and the Nation*, pp. 134–47.

39. T.H.S. Escott, *England: Its People, Polity and Pursuits*, 2 volumes, London, 1885, vol. 2, pp. 417–18; *The Yorkshireman*, 11 October 1884.

40. See, for example, Timothy Finn, *Pub Games of England*, London, 1975.

41. *Yorkshire Post*, 7 February and 2 April 1870.

42. *Yorkshire Post*, 5 March 1870.

43. *Yorkshire Post*, 22 February 1870, 27 January 1900 and 5 February 1870.

44. *Licensing World*, 25 July 1908; *The Licensed Trade News*, 27 August 1910.
45. *Licensing World*, 18 August 1900.
46. See M.A. Kellet, 'The Power of Princely Patronage: Pigeon-Shooting in Victorian Britain', *International Journal of the History of Sport*, vol. 11, number 1, April 1994, pp. 63–85. For the history of firearms legislation in Britain see Joyce Lee Malcolm, *To Keep and Bear Arms*, Harvard, 1994.
47. *Glasgow Herald*, 6 January 1890; *Yorkshire Post*, 23 April 1870.
48. *Glasgow Herald*, 29 July 1870, 24 January 1880 and 9 July 1900. Although the Northumberland and Lancashire county bowls associations had been formed in the 1880s, it wasn't until the 1890s and 1900s that English bowls began to be organised on a county and national basis.
49. *Stirling Observer*, 14 September 1901; *Stirling Journal*, 17 May 1895 and 20 October 1899.
50. *The Scotsman*, 28 July 1830; *Bell's Life in London*, 20 September 1850, 22 August 1851, 29 October 1875.
51. Alan Metcalfe, 'Organised Sport in the Mining Communities of South Northumberland, 1880–1889' in *Victorian Studies*, No. 25, Summer 1982, p. 485.
52. Royal Commission On Licensing (England And Wales) 1929-31, *Report*, London 1932, pp. 1085–6, 21,026-031.
53. W. Bently Capper (ed.), *Licensed Houses and their Management*, London, 1923, p. 21. For a Scottish perspective, see Neil Tranter, *Sport, Economy and Society in Britain 1750-1914*, Cambridge, 1998, p. 37; *Northern Echo*, 26 April 1986; Mass-Observation, *The Pub and the People*, p. 298.
54. Paul Jennings, *The Public House in Bradford, 1770–1970*, Keele, 1995, p. 203; Mass-Observation, *The Pub and the People*, pp. 186–91; Charles Forman, *Industrial Town: Self-Portrait of St Helens in the 1920s*, London, 1978, p. 22; Mass-Observation Archives, 455/Drinking Habits, Box 7: Pub Observations 1947–48, Report by J.G. 21 June 1947 and 'Report on the Influence of Football', J.G. 7 April 1948; *The Cricketer Spring Annual*, London, 1938, p. 49.
55. Mass-Observation, *The Pub and the People*, p. 42 and p. 135; Spike Milligan, 'Foreword' to Peter Bills, *Passion in Exile. 100 Years of London Irish RFC*, Edinburgh, 1998, p. 12. For a discussion on the pub and masculinity see Andrew Davies 'Leisure in the "Classic Slum" 1900–1939' in Andrew Davies and Steven Fielding (eds), *Workers' Worlds: Cultures and Communities in Manchester and Salford 1880–1939*, Manchester, 1992, and Valerie Hey, *Patriarchy and Pub Culture*, London, 1986.
56. *The Licensed Victualler and Catering Trades Journal*, 13 June 1900.
57. *The Licensed Victualler and Catering Trades Journal*, 4 April 1900.
58. Mass-Observation, *The Pub and the People*, p. 25; Royal Commission on Licensing (England and Wales) 1929-31, *Report*, London 1931, p. 1201.
59. Capper, *Licensed Houses and their Management*, vol. 3, p. 21.
60. *The Citizen* (Gloucester), 16 February 1954; *The Licensed Victualler and Catering Trades Journal*, 18 April 1900.

61. Metcalfe, 'Organised Sport in the Mining Communities of South Northumberland', pp. 469–95; *Bridge of Allan Reporter*, 20 August 1858; we are indebted to Dr Neil Tranter for this reference and subsequent references to the *Stirling Journal* and *Stirling Observer*.
62. Metcalfe, 'Organised Sport in the Mining Communities of South Northumberland', p. 485; *The Licensed Victualler and Catering Trades Journal*, 9 May 1900; Tony Flynn, *A History of the Pubs of Eccles*, Manchester, undated, p. 31.
63. Wilson, *Alcohol and the Nation*, p. 141.
64. Mass-Observation, *The Pub and the People*, p. 295; *Caterer and Hotel Keeper*, 7 September 1957.
65. *Stirling Journal*, 20 September 1878.
66. See John Lowerson, 'Angling' in Tony Mason (ed.), *Sport in Britain. A Social History*, Cambridge, 1989, p. 27.
67. Brian Harrison, 'Pubs' in H.J. Dyos and M. Wolff (eds), *The Victorian City: Images and Realities*, London, 1973, p. 173.
68. J. Fairfax Blakeborough, 'The Trade and Art' in *Licensing World*, 4 June 1908.
69. These articles are collected in *Lawful Games on Licensed Premises*, London, undated, [c1900].
70. Quoted in Mark Clapson, *A Bit Of A Flutter, Popular Gambling And English Society c1823-1961*, Manchester, 1992, p. 45. See also Mass-Observation, *The Pub and the People*, pp. 262–5.
71. Bently Capper, *Licensed Houses and their Management*, vol. 3, p. 22.
72. Bessie Beed, *Seventy Years Behind Bars*, London, 1984, quoted in Peter Haydon, *The English Pub*, London, 1994, p. 286.
73. Forman, *Industrial Town*, p. 200.
74. Scott A.G.M. Crawford, 'Coursing' in *Encyclopedia of World Sport*, Oxford, 1996, pp. 85–7.
75. See *Ipswich Evening Star*, 14 February 1959, *Essex Chronicle*, 16 September 1966 and the *Kent and Sussex Courier*, 8 July 1949.
76. Arthur Taylor, *The Guinness Book of Traditional Pub Games*, London, 1992, p. 18. For the 1908 story, see Richard Boston, *Beer and Skittles*, London, 1976, p. 148 and compare with *Lawful Games on Licensed Premises*.
77. Mass-Observation Archives, File Report FR 2505, 'Mutual Aid and the Pub', August 1947.

2

A Thirsty Business: The Drinks Industry and Sport

For as long as there has been a brewing industry in Britain, it has had deep links with British sporting life. The great brewing families themselves had long and intimate connections with sport. The very nature of the trade, with its reliance on agriculture for its basic ingredients, linked it closely with rural life and its recreations. The high social status which brewing's wealth conferred upon the upper echelons of the industry also gave many of its successful practitioners the opportunity to indulge their love of field and other sports. In the first half of the nineteenth century, Harvey Combe of Combe Delderfield was widely known for not letting the demands of his brewery interfere too heavily with his interest in horse racing and field sports; Reid Brewery's William Wigram developed a reputation as an outstanding huntsman during the same period.[1] These links with the turf and the field continued well into the twentieth century – the Whitbread family in particular became well known for their long and abiding passion for horse racing. In the mid-1920s, the young Bill Whitbread, who was to become chairman of the company from 1944 to 1971, rode twice in the Grand National, and was also well known for his success as a polo player, yachtsman and field sportsman. At a less exalted level Barras Reed, the founding managing director of Newcastle Breweries, proudly boasted before his death in 1936 that to celebrate his 75th birthday he had shot seven stags in one day. [2]

The identification of the brewers with rural sports has long been highlighted by the symbolism used in their corporate logos. For example, the distinctive cockerel of the Courage logo was extensively researched among customers in 1949 to decide whether pub-goers preferred the cockerel dressed for fighting (trimmed) or not (untrimmed), despite a century having passed since cockfighting was legal. Perhaps the most evocative of this type of imagery is the red-coated huntsman of Joshua Tetley & Son. Conceived in the 1920s as Tetley's began to expand beyond their traditional West Yorkshire base, the logo is the epitome of rural England, ignoring the fact that the brewery was situated in the heart of urban, industrial Leeds. Such was the appeal of the image that for many years Tetley's shared it with the Dorchester brewer, Eldridge Piper, at first unwittingly and then by mutual consent.[3]

By the mid-nineteenth century the brewers' sporting interests had begun to extend beyond the traditional rural sports. The Walkers of North London were one of many brewing families which developed links with cricket in the early decades of the century. They were instrumental in the establishment of Middlesex County Cricket Club and invited many of the period's leading players to appear at their own ground at Southgate. V.E. Walker captained the Gentlemen against the Players and in 1859 scored a century and took all ten wickets for England against Surrey, while his two brothers respectively captained Middlesex and played for Oxford University. Richard Daft, himself a publican at the Trent Bridge Inn for a short time, was one of the more prominent professionals of the day who benefited from the Walkers' patronage.[4] C.F. Tetley, for many years senior partner of the Leeds-based family brewers, was an official of the Leeds Clarence Cricket Club from the 1870s, and played a prominent role in the building and establishment of Headingley as a major cricket and rugby stadium. He also managed to combine the chairmanship of Leeds Cricket, Football and Athletic Company, the owners of Headingley and the professional Leeds rugby league club, with presidency of Headingley rugby union club, and became a noted supporter of amateur sport.[5] Henry Mitchell, son of the founder of the Mitchell side of Mitchell and Butler, was a noted amateur athlete in the 1880s and the driving force behind Mitchell St George's Football Club. The scions of the Morse family, who controlled Norwich's Steward and Patterson brewery for more than a century, were possibly more distinguished for their achievements as sporting gentlemen than as brewers – Charles played for England at cricket in 1849, George was a noted mountaineer who became president of the Alpine Club in 1926 and Arthur became president of Norfolk County Cricket Club after World War Two.[6] At a local level, the example of J.P. Mangor, the managing director of the Redruth Brewery in Cornwall who provided the ground and a pavilion for the town's cricket club, was repeated across the country.[7]

In Wales, brewing families quite naturally developed their sporting interests through rugby. For example, the Phillips family played a prominent role in the formation of the Newport club in the 1870s. Thomas Phillips sold his Burton brewery to Trumans in 1874 and bought the Dock Road Brewery in Newport. His two sons allegedly took a rugby ball with them and the following year helped to found the town's rugby team. The Hancock family of Cardiff, one of Wales's biggest brewers, played an even more important role in the early history of Welsh rugby. Frank Hancock, who later became managing director of the business, captained both Cardiff and Wales in the 1880s and, of his nine brothers, Philip played for England on four occasions and toured South Africa with the 1891 visiting British side, Ernest played for Cardiff and five others turned out for the Somerset county side. It was allegedly Frank's outstanding skills as a three-quarter that led to Cardiff inventing the four three-quarters system for which Welsh national sides became so famous: such was his talent that the selection committee felt that they couldn't leave him or any of the other three three-quarters out of the side, so they dropped a forward and henceforth played with four.[8] In the 1920s and 1930s three sons of the Beamish stout-brewing family in Cork played for London Irish rugby union club, with two, Charles and George, representing Ireland.[9] This tradition of the sons of brewers establishing a reputation as sportsmen as a prelude to their careers in the business continued into the latter half of the twentieth century, most notably by Piers Courage, who spent three years as a Formula One driver, finishing second in the 1969 Monaco and US Grands Prix, before being killed when his car spun out of control during the 1970 Dutch Grand Prix.

In spending their early manhood in pursuit of sporting rather than business success, the scions of brewing families were following a path trod by many other young men of their class and status. But whereas other careers would take them away from their youthful pursuits, brewing was an industry in which sporting culture was a vital element of its lifeblood. This direct personal involvement of brewers and their sons in sport, especially cricket and horse racing, highlights the fact that, unlike that of pubs, the brewers' relationship with sport was, until the late nineteenth century, generally one of patronage rather than direct commercial exploitation. Financial support for particular clubs and sports was seen as part of the brewer's wider social role in their local community, especially when faced with the growing necessity to counter the temperance movement and its Liberal supporters in Parliament at the end of the nineteenth century. In this, many brewers were simply fulfilling the role they ascribed to themselves as good Tories, helping to maintain the supposedly age-old relationships of duty and obligation between the classes. That many brewers were unaware of or reluctant to exploit the commercial opportunities afforded by the sporting boom of the 1880s and 1890s was demonstrated by the board of Mitchell's in Birmingham, which in 1888 decided it was not worth issuing an advertising card featuring 'Foot Ball' fixtures, despite the fact that their works football side was at that time attaining a national reputation for itself.[10] The presentation of cups and medals to the winners of local competitions, such as the silver shield which Mitchell's presented to the Birmingham and District Cricket League in 1887, was seen as part of an employer's obligation to those he employed or worked with.[11]

The same paternalistic sense of duty underlay the brewers' provision of sports facilities for their employees. The breweries were among the first to organise sports clubs for the benefit of their employees. Unsurprisingly, given the links that many brewing families had with cricket, it was logical that it would be the most popular game played by employees' sports teams. By the 1880s, a number of breweries had formed cricket teams for their employees. Tetley's first cricket side had been established in the 1870s, had folded in 1881 apparently due to problems obtaining a ground, but was resurrected in 1891. Initially it had only been open to manual workers at the brewery, but by the mid-1890s this restriction had been lifted and clerical staff allowed to play. By the turn of the century, when the club was sharing Hunslet rugby league club's Parkside ground, it had become a significant force in local cricket.[12] In Birmingham, the employee cricket team of Mitchell's, who took over Butler's Crown Brewery in 1892 to become Mitchells and Butlers, played their first match in 1882 against the employees of Bourneville chocolate works, eventually becoming regular champions of the Birmingham and District League.[13] The firm was also a pioneer in the formation of works' football teams, largely due to the enthusiasm for the game of Henry Mitchell, heir to the brewing family. He had formed a works' side, Mitchells St George's, in 1887, which rapidly gained a national reputation. In 1889 the club was acknowledged as Birmingham's third football power after Aston Villa and West Bromwich Albion and joined the Football Alliance, an early precursor to the Second Division of the Football League, which also included Newton Heath, Small Heath, Grimsby Town and Sheffield Wednesday. The club's rapid transformation from works' team to semi-professional status appears to have been due almost entirely to 'an enthusiastic president with a long money bag', as *Athletic News* put it but, despite this, it struggled to attract crowds in four figures and was disbanded in 1892, eventually reforming at a less exalted level as Birmingham St George's.[14]

Despite the growth of brewery employees' individual sports teams in the late nineteenth and early twentieth centuries, it was not until after the First World War that multi-sports clubs became commonplace and cemented their place in brewery workplace culture. This was part of a general movement by employers to offer greater welfare provision to their workers in the wake of the war and the Russian Revolution. As a historian of Mitchells and Butlers put it in 1929, 'no enterprising firm which aspires to be in the van of progress or which is alive to its own best interests can afford to neglect welfare work for its employees. For, as health means good work, and recreation means fitness and contentment, welfare is a very efficient synonym for prosperity in every sense of the word.'[15] Barclay Perkins' staff magazine was similarly explicit in 1922 when it pointed to sport's 'value to comradeship' and role in 'moulding national character' in order to persuade staff to attend its second annual August bank holiday sports day.[16] Most breweries threw themselves and their money enthusiastically at the new vogue for providing sports facilities for their employees. Watney's even called their staff magazine *Beer and Skittles*. One of the first fruits of this collective response was the creation of the London Breweries' Amateur Sports Association, the London Breweries' Football League and other competitions which created a focus for the inter-works competition in the capital. Watney's staff sports club was formed in 1919 and its grounds at Mortlake became a model for employee sports facilities.[17] In 1923 Truman's followed suit, paying £2,100 for a 6-acre site and employing a full-time groundsman at 50 shillings per week.[18] The same year Worthington paid £1,200 for a 12-acre site in Burton on Trent for their newly formed sports club, which included cricket, football, tennis and bowls clubs. The pattern was repeated by breweries in Scotland too; William Younger's – who supplied their manual labourers with three free pints of beer per day – expanded their employee's facilities significantly in the 1920s, building on the success of their rifle range in the pre-war era when the company provided ammunition 'at especially cheap rates' to staff.[19]

Others were not so enthusiastic however. In 1928 an employee of Tetley's asked the brewery to organise a sports day similar to that organised by fellow Yorkshire brewers Bentley's, but was rebuffed with the reply that there was nowhere to hold it. By 1930, a sports club had been formed, apparently by the employees themselves, and recruited 450 members, forcing the directors to change their approach and declare that they 'were ready and willing to help forward any scheme for health-giving recreation and would consider favourably any properly formulated scheme submitted to them'.[20] Although the tone of the response suggests suspicion of the venture, it is possible that Tetley's reluctance to promote a sports club was also due to the costs involved in setting up and running such a facility. To some extent, the expense of sports facilities was inflated by the competitive pride which many breweries took in the size and condition of their grounds. Watney's extensive grounds at Mortlake were comparable with, if not better than, many professional sports grounds, being used for the annual English Bowling Championships in the 1960s. Mitchells and Butlers grounds at Smethwick, had a similar reputation, boasting three cricket pitches, two football pitches, nine tennis courts, five bowling greens and one netball pitch. In 1931 George's in Bristol purchased a 6-acre site for use by their staff, despite an unsympathetic local council.[21] The desire to emulate these paragons of work-based recreation was highlighted by Truman's, who, in addition to their initial 1922 outlay, spent another £1,850 buying tennis courts and enlarging their sports facilities in 1934 and 1935. Even as late as 1937, Reading-based brewers Simonds spent £3,000 buying suitable grounds and another £2,500 bringing them up to their required standards.[22]

As Worthington's discovered, the initial start-up costs were only the beginning of the necessary expenditure. They spent an additional £882 in the year after the acquisition of their ground equipping it with tennis courts, bowling greens, dressing rooms and a pavilion; the following year they employed a full-time cricket professional. It was hoped that at least the football section would become self-supporting by 1925 but this turned out to be a forlorn hope, as the sports club as a whole only survived due to annual subsidies of no less than £200 throughout the next decade and the cricket professional's wages also had to be subsidised when the club's canteen takings proved insufficient to support him during the winter months.[23] Indeed, the subsidies continued to rise and in 1934 the newly merged Bass and Worthington sports clubs were given £515 to continue their operations. This continued until 1940, when a donation of £212 proved to be the last until the end of the Second World War.[24] The subsidies continued after the end of the war, rising to £800 by 1956. Perhaps symbolically for the rest of the trade, in 1960 Simond's gave up any hope of their staff sports and social club being self-sustaining and decided to abandon subscriptions and simply grant an ongoing annual donation of £1,000 to cover its activities.[25]

Sport and the Marketing of Alcohol

The seeds of the commercial exigencies which were to undermine this paternalism were sown in the rush to the stock market of the mid-1880s and the subsequent scramble for tied houses which enormously increased the competitive pressures facing the industry. The contemporary successes of national retailers and the growth of advertising were lessons not lost on the drinks industry: the need to increase profits and market share meant that techniques of marketing were rapidly taken on board. Although brewers had advertised in newspapers since the end of the eighteenth century, many of these were aimed at the trade itself and not undertaken in any systematic way. Indeed, it wasn't until 1856, a full sixty-four years after the brewery was founded, that Joshua Tetley saw the need to publish its first newspaper advertisement.[26] The development of national retail networks of breweries and their tied houses carried with it the need for distinctive corporate identities and product differentiation, brought about by the need to attract and retain customers, which saw brands, trade marks and advertising assume great importance in the last decades of the century. And the fact that the masses flocking to watch and play sport in this period were almost without exception consumers of alcohol was not lost on the drinks industry. One of the most ubiquitous advertisements of the 1880s, and for the best part of a century afterwards, was that for Grant's Morella Cherry Brandy, which quickly sought to identify itself as an aid to the sportsman; 'Much Patronised by Football Players' and 'The Sportsman's Quality for Open-Air Exercise' being two of its more direct if somewhat artless slogans of the 1890s and 1900s respectively. Few match-day programmes, whether for football or rugby, were complete without an advertisement for the local brewer or beer. Cards detailing the fixtures of local teams and featuring advertisements for the brewery producing the card, as rejected by Mitchell's, became commonplace in the 1890s – and such was their perceived importance by some brewers that by 1932 William McEwan in Scotland was spending more on producing football fixture cards than on any other form of marketing. Advertising in local sports handbooks also became ubiquitous – the official guide for the Hull and District Rugby Union for the 1895/96 season carried a one-line advertisement for Hull Brewery across the top of every page, each bearing a message such as 'Drink the Hull Brewery Company's Beer', 'Special Working Men's Mild Ale' and 'Beer is the National English Drink'. In contrast, one of the more incongruous marketing initiatives of the period was Krug's special 1889 Champagne Cuvée, featuring a football on the label, which was produced to mark Preston North End's double winning season of 1888/89.[27]

It was not only those sports patronised by the working classes which attracted the attention of the drinks industry's early marketing departments. The tremendous growth in golf and tennis clubs in the 1890s and 1900s was not simply due to the sporting and networking facilities offered by the new clubs but was also driven by the fact that they were also exclusive drinking establishments largely free from the interference of the licensing laws. Magazines such as *Golf Illustrated* offered wine and spirits manufacturers and merchants ample opportunity to advertise their wares not only to individuals but to club managers and stewards too. Although brewers are largely absent as advertisers in magazines for sports seen as middle class, it is noticeable that distillers of whisky and gin used middle-class sports journals to make exactly the same claims for the health-giving and sport-aiding properties of their products as were made for beer. Colonel Bogey whisky asserted that it was a 'most stimulating tonic for golfers', Rose's claimed that their lime juice liqueur was 'especially recommended to Huntsmen, Golfers and Sportsmen generally', and Cambus proclaimed that their whisky was 'highly approved by the medical profession'. The importance of alcohol to the culture and rituals of golf and similar sports can be seen in the appeals made by advertisers to their audience: Grant's advertised their sloe gin by pointing out that it was allegedly 'in great request for the flask by sportsmen', highlighting the centrality of the hip-flask to middle-class outdoor pursuits, while by 1910 John Harvey of Bristol was even producing a 'Golf Blend Scotch' which was advertised using an illustration of four golfers entering 'the nineteenth hole'. It may well be the case that the use of the phrase 'nineteenth hole' as a euphemism for the clubhouse, which had originated in the United States, was brought into common parlance through its use in advertising at this time.[28]

Sport's importance to the marketing of alcohol, and beer in particular, was highlighted most strikingly by the role played by the brewers in the financing of the 'football boom' of the 1890s and early 1900s. The tremendous growth in football crowds, spurred by the formation of the Football League in 1888 and the huge popularity of the FA Cup, meant that many clubs needed substantial capital investment as they sought to improve their grounds through the building of new grandstands and enhancing of other facilities. The financial support of breweries was crucial to many clubs' expansion – and was often acknowledged by the name of the brewer being painted in large letters across the roof of a stand: one of Barnsley's stands was known as 'the Brewery Stand' and, in a variation on the theme, Aston Villa had 'Mitchells & Butlers Good Honest Beer' running around the overhanging lip of a stand roof. The brewers made no bones about the reasons for their support: capital was provided 'in view of the benefit to the trade of customers in the neighbourhood' was how the board of William Younger justified its expenditure when the company bought shares in Hearts in 1905. Wolverhampton Wanderers moved into Molineux thanks to the help of the ground's owners, Northampton Breweries, who also built a stand, covered standing areas, dressing rooms and an office for an annual rent of £50. West Bromwich Albion depended on loans from Mitchells & Butlers to keep afloat in the later 1900s.[29] Oldham Athletic's bid for Football League status in 1907 was successful in large part because the previous year J.W. Lees, the local brewer, had provided the club with a permanent home at an old rugby ground which they owned and which became known as Boundary Park.[30]

Other clubs owed their very existence to a brewer's support. The most notable example was Liverpool, whose birth was entirely due to the brewer John Houlding. Houlding had been a crucial figure in Everton's rise to success in the 1880s, when he provided the club with its then ground at Anfield and changing room facilities in his Sandon Hotel. The club's success in the fledgling Football League saw him attempt to extract maximum value from his investment by raising the rent he charged the club for the ground and refusing to surrender his right to sell refreshments on match days. After the club turned down his offer to sell Anfield to them for £6,000, he forced them to leave and founded a new club to play on the ground: Liverpool FC, which was effectively controlled for most of its early years by Houlding and three other local brewers.

Manchester United's debt to the drinks trade was only marginally less. Plagued by financial problems in the 1890s, Newton Heath FC finally went into liquidation in 1902 and were bought for £500 by J.H. Davies, the chairman of Manchester Breweries. Renamed Manchester United by its new owner, the club became an appendage of the brewery. Its seven-strong board consisted of Davies and six other employees of the brewery, including team manager J.J. Bentley, who was unique in that his position with the brewery was a consequence of his role at the club, rather than vice versa as was the case with his fellow directors. The club not only owed its existence to Davies, but also its ground. In 1909 he provided the £60,000 which allowed the club to move from Clayton to Old Trafford and equip their new ground with outstanding facilities for the time. Like Houlding, Davies' interest in the club was not simply due to a love of sport: an FA enquiry in 1910 discovered that he received £740 rent from the club for land it did not use. The importance of the link between a football club and its local brewery at this time was further underlined across the city, when Manchester City's attempts to move from its Hyde Road ground were frustrated by objections from Chester's Brewery, who felt that its substantial financial support for the club over the years would go to waste if the team moved to a stadium away from the brewer's traditional customer base.[31]

This type of symbiotic relationship between brewery and football club was also demonstrated by that of Benskins Brewery and Watford. As part of the club's campaign for acceptance into the Football League's newly formed Division Three South, the brewery bought its Cassio Road ground after the lease expired in 1916. Unfortunately, the ground failed to meet the minimum standards for the new division, so Benskins bought Vicarage Road for the club in 1922 and loaned them £12,000 to bring it up to scratch. The price of this support was steep: the brewery demanded 10 per cent of the gate receipts and that its representatives on the board of directors should have the power of veto over major decisions, including transfers. The club was hit by a financial crisis in 1926 but, after some initial hesitation, it was rescued by the brewery which paid off a number of debts. Unsurprisingly, for many years the club was known as 'the Brewers', with or without the possessive apostrophe.[32]

Benskins' support for Watford was not unusual. Simonds' brewery provided similar, if less publicly obvious, support to Reading FC throughout the inter-war years. In 1926 the brewery loaned the club £5,000 to build a new grandstand to be paid back by annual instalments of 25 per cent of the takings from the new stand or £1,250, whichever was higher. In 1930 Simonds' board of directors decided to make a further loan of another £5,000, secured on the new grandstand, in part so that the club could repay a £1,400 debt to their bankers, to be repaid at the same rate as the old loan. The following year, the minimum annual payment was reduced to £500 a year. By the end of the 1934 season the club was in such dire straits that the brewery suspended repayments on the remaining £3,000 of the loan. Despite the obvious financial paralysis gripping the club, another loan of £1,200 was granted in October 1935 at a reduced rate of interest. Six months later a further loan of £2,300 was made. It was not until March 1938 that the club was able to repay a substantial part of their loans with a payment of £1,500 to Simonds.

In effect, the brewery acted as the principal banker to the club from the late 1920s onwards, particularly after it had loaned the club money with which to pay off its bank debt. Although many breweries had bought nominal amounts of shares in their local clubs since the 1880s, such transactions were clearly of a different order. Many of the loans it made were not financially beneficial to Simonds yet the importance of the link with football was suffic-ient to offset any possible risk involved in the loan. It is probable that many other breweries had similar relationships with clubs in their areas, especially during the depression of the 1930s, yet the partial nature of most breweries' records of dealing with sports clubs and the fact that much brewery business at this level was conducted by word of mouth means that documentary evidence is difficult to find. The scrupulous attention to detail of the Simonds' board of directors fortunately has left us with a much fuller account of the financial intricacies of the relationship between local brewers and football clubs.[33]

A major reason for Benskins' and Simonds', and doubtless other brewers', forbearance with their local clubs in the 1920s was due to the poor state of the drinks trade as a whole after the war and the necessity to make the most of any opportunity to retain and attract customers. The problems faced by the industry in the 1900s had been not alleviated by the ending of the First World War. If anything, they appeared to have been exacerbated. In part due to Lloyd George's rhetoric – 'Drink is doing us more damage in the war than all the German submarines put together,' he declared in February 1915 – and a real fear that drunkenness would interfere with war production, a range of draconian measures were introduced during the war that severely curtailed pub opening hours, increased the price of beer and reduced its alcoholic content. These remained in force after the war ended, and together with the continued expansion of other sources of leisure, the trade faced even greater problems in the inter-war period than in the decades immediately before the war. Con-sumption of both beer and spirits continued to fall. As the historian of George's in Bristol comments, 'from a national perspective the inter-war period presents a dismal picture for brewing, as aggregate and per capita consumption of beer continued to fall'.[34]

The industry responded by consolidating through a new round of takeovers and also by embarking on an unprecedented level of advertising. Aside from the 1926 merger of Bass and Worthington, the two biggest Burton brewers, most of the acquisitions and mergers took place at the middle and lower levels of the industry, as those companies too weak to compete or still suffering from huge debts incurred during the rush to acquire pubs in the 1890s and 1900s found themselves picked off by the likes of Ind Coope, Simonds and Watney, Combe, Reid. Consequently, the need to increase sales and market share led to a significant rise in the level of advertising both individually and, for the first time, collectively too.

The use of national advertising was inspired by the success of the 'Guinness Is Good For You' campaign which was launched across Britain by the Irish brewer in February 1929. The first press advertisement claimed that 'Guinness builds strong muscles. It feeds exhausted nerves. It enriches the blood. Doctors affirm that Guinness is a valuable restorative after influenza and other weakening illnesses.' Like many other food and drink marketing campaigns of the time, it appealed directly to contemporary fears of declining health and fitness. In 1932 the campaign was developed further with the introduction of the slogan 'Guinness for Strength,' which made a more direct appeal to sporting instincts by featuring athletic motifs. In subsequent years the campaign was broadened to feature specific sports, enjoying an especially fruitful relationship with cricket, as one of its more poetic advertisements highlighted:

> You're out of luck, your score was a duck.
> From fielding your feet are quite sore.
> Now by missing a catch, you've just lost the match.
> What is it a lovely day for?
> Lovely Day For A Guinness.[35]

The resonance of the Guinness campaign led the Brewers' Society to reconsider their previous reluctance to advertise collectively. A generic advertising campaign for beer had been suggested as early as 1920 by the *Brewers' Journal* but it was a horrifying 34 per cent drop in the consumption of beer and a corresponding fall in profit levels between 1929 and 1933 that finally persuaded the brewers to engage in collective action to revive the market. The problem faced by the industry was captured in June 1933 by Sir Edgar Sanders, the President of the Brewers' Society:

the chief customers of the public house today are the elderly and middle-aged men. Unless you can attract the younger generation to take the place of the older men, there is no doubt that we shall have to face a steadily falling consumption of beer . . . I am not saying that the present beer drinker should drink more, but rather that we want new customers. We want to get the beer-drinking habit instilled into thousands, almost millions, of young men who do not at present know the taste of beer.

In a speech which was to be reprinted by countless temperance publications over the next fifty years as evidence of the nefarious designs of the brewers, he pointed to the success of soap manufacturers who used film stars to advertise their products and suggested that there were 'plenty of footballers, plenty of cricketers, plenty of prizefighters' who could help beer in the same way.[36] Consequently, in the summer of 1933 the Brewers' Society appointed a committee of the Brewers' Society led by Whitbread managing director Sidney Neville to initiate the development of a campaign, which was finally unveiled in December of that year. Designed by the London Press Agency, the campaign unashamedly sought to exploit beer's traditional associations with health, strength and sport by proclaiming 'Beer is Best'.[37]

The theme of the campaign was that beer was best for healthy living, sporting activity, conviviality and just about everything else, typified by an advertisement later in the campaign which showed two images of the same man, one of him working in a shop contrasted with an image of him camping in the country. The copy, complete with lame pun, read 'How can a man like you keep fit for this? This pints [sic] the way. Beer is best'. The image of a shot putter was used to demonstrate beer's strength-giving properties. By the late 1930s the campaign was drawing explicit links with the theme of military preparedness with its 'For an A1 people, beer is best' headline. The originality of the campaign lay not so much in its message – which was basically a repetition of the Guinness campaign – but in the modern marketing techniques used to get the message across to the public. The slogan appeared on newspaper and magazine advertisements, advertising hoardings, posters, beer mats, calendars and almost any other printed surface on which it was possible to advertise, becoming a topic for discussion and comment in itself. Interestingly, Sanders' vision of using prominent sportsmen to advertise beer didn't come to pass, at least not until after the war, possibly because the illustrative style of the advertisements proved to be very popular and also perhaps because a direct association with alcohol may not have been perceived as being wholly respectable by the footballing authorities – especially after the temperance movement had responded to the campaign by defacing the posters by writing the words 'left alone' after 'beer is best'.

Nevertheless, in bare statistical terms the campaign appeared to have been a success, beer consumption rising by over 37 per cent in the six years following the start of the campaign. However, this rise was almost certainly not unconnected with the general recovery of the British economy from the mid-1930s, so the real economic impact of the campaign is difficult to quantify. What it most definitely did do, however, was to persuade the brewers of the efficacy of advertising. Spurred by the success of the Guinness and beer campaigns, each of which was spending an average of over £100,000 a year on advertising from 1933 to 1938, spending by the industry on advertising rose to new levels during the 1930s, with Bass, probably the strongest brand name in the trade after Guinness, in the vanguard.[38]

Although the main audience for the 'Beer is Best' campaign was the working classes to whom beer was the traditional drink of choice, the brewers also used it in an attempt to broaden beer's appeal to the middle classes. Film actors Gertrude Lawrence and Ronald Squire appeared in advertisements drinking beer in prestigious London hotels and specialised campaigns ran in golf and cricket magazines. Copywriters went to great lengths to entice drinkers and were not above using doggerel poetry to demonstrate how beer was best:

> Before the largest crowd he's cool –
> He hits a mighty ball;
> He doesn't top or slice or pull,
> And clean out-drives them all.
> He's born to play a champion's role –
> The signs are very clear . . .!
> And always at the 19th hole
> You'll find he'll . . . ask for beer.[39]

This focus on golf and cricket was also due to the continued growth in the number of licensed clubs and the sharp increase in sales of bottled beer, which became an increasingly important market for the trade in the 1930s and by 1939 accounted for 30 per cent of all beer sold. It was not coincidental that it was the brewers which specialised in bottled beer, such as Guinness, and its smaller rival William Younger, who were among the leading advertisers of the period. Indeed, much of Younger's advertising echoed that of its Irish rival – 'To Get Fitter, Get Younger' being one of its more memorable slogans – while the visual themes of its advertisements included a cricket bat whose shadow resembled a beer bottle and an over-par golf scorecard which, claimed the copywriter, was a good enough reason for a beer. McEwan's advertising throughout the 1930s featured sportsmen who had discovered the benefits of their bottled beer under the simple headline 'The Reviver'.

But the legacy of the importance of clubs to the industry was not simply a rise in the level of advertising and bad puns. The demands of the clubs had an impact on the way in which beer was brewed. Unlike the pub, where demand was relatively constant throughout the week, most golf, cricket or tennis clubs did the vast bulk of their trade at weekends. This meant that a great deal of beer was being wasted as it went out of condition when left unused for the best part of a week. In 1936 East Sheen Lawn Tennis Club asked Watney's, their supplier, if there was anything which could be done about the problem. Possibly at the suggestion of Bert Hussey, a brewer at Watney's who also happened to be a member of the club, the brewery gave them a barrel of their new pasteurised beer, Red Barrel, a type of India Pale Ale which, because it was meant for export overseas, had a much longer life. The beer proved to be a success with clubs and drinkers alike, but in the eyes of many it marked the beginning of a decline in the quality of English beer: in the 1960s and 1970s Watney's Red Barrel became, in the words of pub historian Peter Haydon, 'synonymous with all that was abysmal'.[40]

In contrast, wines and spirits suffered no disadvantages in a club environment. The consumption of spirits had declined in the inter-war years, although not as much as beer, and the distillers followed the brewers in increasing their advertising in the 1930s, albeit on an individual rather than a collective basis. The close association between spirit drinking and middle-class sporting identity was keen reflected by the distillers' advertising campaigns. MacKinley's advertised their VOB scotch with the slogan 'During the drive at the 18th tee – don't forget, at the 19th, there's VOB', while Haig promoted their whisky with cartoon golfers whose frustration at their efforts inevitably led them to the 19th and a glass of Haig. Black & White whisky used illustrations of idealised rustic village green cricket to promote their label: 'After the best of games, the best o' whisky' ended one advertisement in *The Cricketer*. But it was Johnny Walker's scotch which sought to make its brand synonymous with golf and cricket with a series of advertisements throughout the 1930s. As early as 1930 the company had offered a free bottle of scotch to anyone getting a verifiable hole in one and it advertised itself as the greeting for 'the weary golfer': 'everyone knows the 19th hole. That's the last hole of the day. It's the "hole" you're going to make in a bottle of Johnny Walker. This is where you follow the example of all good golfers since 1820.' It used the same style of advertising in the cricket press. It proclaimed itself '1820 Not Out', a reference to the date of the company's foundation and advised readers that 'a gruelling stretch in the slips or a heated "bodyline" discussion in the Pavilion call for a cooling, refreshing, stimulating beverage – Johnny Walker'. Another advertisement asked what the difference was between a cricket ball and a good whisky: '"a cricket ball," said Johnny Walker, taking one in his hand, "has got a seam – you can see and feel where the join comes. But a good whisky like Johnny Walker is somewhat like a billiard ball, perfectly round, perfectly smooth . . ."'[41]

The Johnny Walker campaigns, and others which followed similar themes such as those for Black & White whisky, were markedly different from those which had gone before and also from those used by the brewers. The advertisements made no claims about any supposed health-giving qualities for their products; there was no attempt to show that they were any aid to personal fitness. Instead, they appealed directly to the social, relaxing attributes of alcohol and to the spectator as well as the player. In this they reflected a growing openness about the hitherto implicit appeal of the golf club: the opportunities it afforded for drinking. This had been brought to the fore during the 1929 Royal Commission on Licensing when the National Golf Clubs' Protection Association, which had been founded to protest against the 1921 restrictions on club opening hours, had argued that clubs should not be bound by the same rules as pubs. Although their representative, Frank Holroyd, had argued that the sale of alcoholic refreshment was entirely subordinate to the playing of golf and that, unlike pubs, clubs were not dependent on it, his argument was fatally undermined when he was asked by a member of the Commission if golfers would play 'without intoxicating liquor?' 'I do not think you will find many of them who would care to do so,' was his honest reply.[42]

Many golf advertisements explicitly built on the appeal of the 19th hole while those for cricket were based on the pleasures of watching and discussing the game. Underlying the advertisers' attempts to appeal to the non-player or recreational player was the evocation of a nostalgia for the supposedly simpler times of the past, free of economic depression, industrial unrest and overseas threats: Johnny Walker rarely missed an opportunity to refer to 1820. But it was Black & White's advertising in particular which sought to evoke an ideal of a rural 'Merrie England', most notably in the text of a 1938 advertisement:

> Says the oldest inhabitant – 'It be'ant my place to say as 'ow we could a done better in my time. Our lads takes their knowcks and enjoys it. If they wins, they wins and if they loses, they lose. We mayn't know so much about cricket as the pros, but we know what a good afternoon's play deserves. Win or lose, we allus finishes up at Manor ower a drop of Squire's whisky . . . that means 'Black & White'.

Another advertisement was even more explicit in its picture of social harmony and mixing through sport and drink:

> 'What I like about cricket,' said the Average Man, 'is its democratic atmosphere. I enjoy arguing the merits of my team just as much with the plumber sitting on my left as with the retired Colonel on the other side. And as likely as not we'll all three adjourn to pick the next Test side over a "Black & White".'[43]

A similar theme was evoked by a 1940s series of advertisements for the Brewers' Society featuring illustrations of idealised country pub life commissioned from members of the Royal Academy that bore the generic headline 'At the Friendly Inn' which appeared in golf magazines of the period. It is important to note that these advertisements were not trying to convince working-class drinkers that they were welcome in what were perceived as being socially exclusive golf or cricket clubs. Their aim was to reassure middle-class readers that they were safe in their assumptions and view of the world. This was not simply due to a shared ideological stance or psychologically-astute advertising: the brewers had an economic interest in encouraging the use of clubs, due not only to their need to sell their products to clubs and also because of the fact that they had made substantial investments in the clubs themselves.

Alcohol and the Rise of Sports Sponsorship

Although it was not unknown for brewers to make loans or donations to clubs before the First World War, the focus of competition in the industry had been on pubs and exploiting the advantages that the new networks of tied houses gave brewers. However, the continuing decline in patterns of consumption after the war meant a greater emphasis on non-traditional outlets, such as bottled beer and clubs: the number of pubs in the UK fell by 10 per cent between 1919 and 1936 while the number of clubs increased by a third between 1925 and 1935.[44] The provision of loans and favourable credit terms in return for being the sole supplier of the club's alcohol needs allowed breweries to effectively 'tie' clubs into their retail network and expand the size of their share of the market. As the report of the 1929 Royal Commission on Licensing delicately noted: 'some sections of the brewing industry have . . . by means more or less direct, lent financial and other assistance towards the formation, with a view to registration, of clubs in which their wares may find an outlet'. [45] This became especially true in the early 1930s, when economic recession hit the industry hard. Thus, for example, in 1930 Truman's loaned £1,000 at 5 per cent to the Boyce Hill Golf Club and also gave them a discount on beer purchases of 7.5 per cent, and over the next decade loaned varying amounts of money to Chatham Civil Service Club, Southend Civil Service Sports Club, the Spurs Supporters' Club and Thornton Heath Sports Club among others. In 1935 a dispute broke out with Ilford Golf Club over the fact that, contrary to an agreement made with the brewery, it had 'from time to time sold nips of Guinness and Worthington'. Truman's request that they stop selling rival brands was turned down because 'restriction of supply would prejudice the success of the club' and eventually a compromise was reached whereby the club provided Truman's with a record of all non-Truman beers purchased.[46] Not all clubs were treated so tolerantly. In 1934 Bass loaned the Mere Golf Club near Manchester £1,000 on condition that not only did they restrict their sales to Bass and Worthington beers but also that their credit period was shortened from three months to one.[47]

The enthusiasm of brewers to lend to clubs did not go unnoticed by sports clubs themselves. Many rugby union clubs also sought loans from brewers in order to enhance their facilities and install the all-important bar; a fairly representative example being Batley Rugby Union Club who in 1935 decided to expand their clubhouse and set up a committee to negotiate a loan with Joshua Tetley & Son.[48] However, in contrast to most sports of the time, the Rugby Football Union had an active policy of providing loans for facilities to its member clubs and this helped to reduce, although not eliminate, the need for rugby clubs to seek brewery finance. In contrast, those sports such as golf which were without a centralised organising body were much more reliant on external largesse and the minutes of the brewers are littered with requests for loans from sports clubs. In general, it appears that breweries tended to make loans or investments only when there was more on offer than a simple return on the money advanced – as can be seen in their support to local football clubs or in the offers of money predicated on exclusive supply deals. Often the advantages were obvious: when in September 1927 Simonds bought 500 one shilling shares in Wembley Stadium it came as no surprise to anyone when shortly afterwards they won the contract to supply the stadium with refreshments.[49]

This tapestry of interlocking commercial deals with clubs and other sporting organisations was extended in the 1940s and 1950s. In 1948 Simonds acted as guarantors for Streatham Park Bowling Club's £1,000 overdraft at Barclay's, a bank which had close links with the brewery: J.H. Simonds had actually joined the bank's board in 1923.[50] Truman's were especially active in developing their network, offering deals to clubs which undercut other brewers; for example, the Fairfield Golf Club in Manchester received an interest-free loan which was to be repaid through a percentage of the value of the Truman's beer it sold, undercutting a rival bid for the club's trade by Tadcaster's Samuel Smith brewery. In the same year, King's Lynn Football Club asked for and received £500 for refurbishments, the only condition being that they agreed to an exclusive seven-year trade deal. Others were not so fortunate: a golf club at Hellesdon near Norwich found their request for a £3,000 loan to build a new clubhouse turned down because their sales of the brewery's beer were a mere seventy-five barrels a year. Indeed, any board discussion of whether to grant a loan or better trade terms was inevitably accompanied by an analysis of the applicant's sales of the brewery's products and the levels of interest shown by its rivals.

Despite the extensive use of marketing and advertising campaigns, in the period between the end of the Second World War and 1960 draught beer consumption fell by 14 per cent and pubs continued to close, although bottled and the newly introduced canned beers grew in popularity, as did wines and spirits. As competition between brewers intensified in the late 1950s, so too did the need to acquire the trade of sports organisations. In 1958 Truman's bought out Lacon's interest in the Norwich Speedway Company to acquire a trade thought to be worth almost 200 barrels a year. Two years later, William Younger's outbid Trumans for the trade of the Alhambra Sports Club, a large snooker club in Manchester, despite the fact that the latter had offered the club a £2,000 loan repayable through a percentage of beer bought from them. In 1961 Hendon Greyhound Track offered Truman's half of their trade, worth 100 barrels annually, in exchange for a £1,000 loan to be paid off by a charge of 10 shillings per barrel sold. In the same year Macclesfield Rugby Union Club received an interest-free loan of £453 to refurbish their clubhouse, repayable at a mere £45 per year. This was to be one of the last formal arrangements with a club to be made by Truman's or any other brewer as the Licensing Act of 1961 explicitly forbade loans being made to a club on condition of a tie being established. Although introduced to protect clubs and stop the big brewers controlling the club trade in the same way as they did the pub trade, it had the immediate effect of making clubs' financial arrangements more precarious, as a number of brewers, Trumans included, inserted clauses into all new loans requiring repayment of the loan on three months' notice if requested.

The 1961 Act was partly a response to the transformation of the industry which was underway, a change comparable to the upheavals of the late-Victorian era. 'Merger Mania' rivaled the rush to the stock market of the late 1880s as the major brewers embarked on a series of takeovers which saw the industry consolidate into a handful of major brewing groups. In 1961 Whitbread merged with Tennent's in Glasgow, marking the start of a decade which saw them 'merge' with another twenty-two breweries. In the same year, Bass took over Mitchells and Butlers and continued to digest a host of others over the following years. In the space of a whirligig eighteen months, Joshua Tetley took over their major Leeds rival Melbourne Breweries, then merged with Lancashire's Walker Cain brewery to form Tetley Walker and subsequently amalgamated with Ind Coope to form what was known from 1962 onwards as Allied Breweries. The pattern of merger and acquisition was repeated across the industry throughout Britain, so much so that by 1967 the top five brewers had increased their share of the industry's total assets to 63 per cent, tripling 1952's total of 21 per cent.[51]

Not surprisingly, this was to have a profound impact on the marketing of beer – and sport was central to these new developments. The consolidation of the industry led to a huge rebranding of pubs, due both to changes in ownership and also to a need to make them more attractive to customers. To broaden their appeal, the names of many pubs were changed to incorporate popular sporting themes. Others had the meanings of their names subtly changed: the Derby Turn in Burton at the junction of the Derby Road had its sign changed to show a horse rounding Tattenham Corner at Epsom, while the Derby Arms in East Sheen found its association with the Earl of Derby discarded in favour of similar imagery.[52] Television advertising grew rapidly too, with sport featuring prominently – Watney's featured a football team drinking in the dressing room after a match and one of the last acts of the 'Beer is Best' campaign was a TV campaign featuring, among others, Denis Law, Bobby Moore, Billy Walker, Tom Graveney, Fred Trueman and the entire Liverpool football team, which ran for three years from 1964.[53] Advertising in sports magazines and related publications increased too, while many drinks manufacturers, inspired by the success of Guinness's publishing of its eponymous book of records from 1955 – which itself had an athletic genesis, the first edition being partially facilitated through the work of British middle-distance runner Chris Chataway who was working at Guinness's Park Royal brewery at the time – ventured into the publishing of sports books. Martini published maps of golf courses from the late 1950s, Worthington produced a guide to coarse fishing and Watney's sponsored a series of books on cricket grounds, bowls, pub games and inland cruising. Guinness even started selling posters of its sport-based advertisements to the public. But perhaps the most important long-term impact of this emphasis on the use of sport as a marketing tool was the emergence of sports sponsorship as a major component of the drinks industry's marketing strategies.

Sports sponsorship was not a new direction for brewers and distillers. Indeed, the support of the old brewing families for cricket and horse racing in the nineteenth century could be considered a precursor of modern sponsorship. Certainly by the early years of the twentieth century a number of breweries were offering trophies to local sporting competitions – in 1906 Mitchells and Butlers paid for a silver shield and medals to be presented annually to the winners of the Birmingham and District Works FA cup competition – but in general these were seen as acts of benevolence towards the local market with no direct commercial outcome.[54] However, the model for modern sponsorship methods, whereby a competition is paid by a sponsor to adopt a brand name, was established during the darts boom of the 1930s. The tremendous popularity of darts was capitalised upon by breweries who saw the popularity of the sport as a means of bringing customers into pubs. Although newspapers, inspired by the example of the *News of the World* in the late 1920s, also sponsored local competitions, it was the breweries who played the major role in sponsoring the explosive growth of the dense thicket of local darts leagues and cups. By 1937 *Darts Weekly News* was proclaiming without fear of contradiction that it was 'the game of a hundred thousand public houses'. In Lancashire, the Taylor Walker league boasted over 117,000 players, while leagues sponsored by Courage, Watney's, Marstons, Barclays and many smaller breweries had hundreds of divisions stretching across boundaries of age, sex and region. By the late 1940s, the Courage League encompassed 500 teams, Taylor Walkers' name was attached to thirty different leagues and, with the exception of one or two competitions attached to local temperance organisations such as the Belfast Temperance League, there was scarcely a darts league without a brewery link.[55] As well as money, which rarely amounted to more than £25 annually, sponsorship also brought with it an order and structure to the sport, including independent, brewery-appointed stewards in some London competitions, for which many darts enthusiasts were grateful:

> in the last few years there has been a revival to such an extent that the smart set has taken to the game. One must remember the brewery companies whose assistance to its recovery has been valuable, with leagues for their houses, and whose teams are subject to observance of strict rules making quite an interesting affair of the game.[56]

The focus of this type of sponsorship had largely been on local regions and driven by the need to attract custom for the brewers' pubs. In contrast, the sponsorship of the Sandown Gold Cup by Whitbread in 1957 marked a new, if for the present somewhat isolated, move into national corporate sponsorship. Whitbread were not the first to sponsor a horse race – in 1947 Simonds had paid £100 to Windsor Racecourse to name a race after the brewery's hop leaf logo, thus inaugurating the 'Hop Leaf Handicap' – but this was the first time that such a well-known name had been attached to a sporting event of such national prominence.[57] Despite the attention gained by the sponsorship – and by Hennessey Brandy's similarly successful backing of horse racing a few years later – it was not until the upheavals of the late 1950s and early 1960s that the importance and value of such sponsorships began to be systematically explored, with the tobacco industry being as keen as their cousins in the drinks trade. The value of such sponsorships was obvious, as Tennent's admitted in their staff magazine when discussing their financial backing of Scotland's national football side: 'To get the same amount of press advertising (not to mention BBC and Radio Clyde) would have cost many thousands of pounds

... our backing of Scotland's world cup squad was patriotism, partly, but also a commercial matter of publicity.'[58]

In the latter half of the 1950s Martini began to sponsor British PGA golf tournaments, a development of their decades-long advertising campaign in the golfing press. In 1961 Truman's made its first foray into sponsorship when it paid £500 to the Greyhound Racing Association to sponsor an annual greyhound race. The same year saw Whitbread extend its involvement in sponsorship but focused on a brand, Mackeson stout, rather than its corporate name, when it began what became known as the Mackeson Trophy, a competition for the top-scoring rugby league teams.[59] In 1965 South African Wines presented prizes to the top performers on that year's South African cricket tour of England. By the late 1960s, it had become commonplace to see sports events bearing the name of a drinks manufacturer or brand. The fact that regulatory controls over the content of advertisements were outlawing claims for alcohol's health-giving properties also increased the need for drinks' manufacturers to find new ways of associating their products with sport and fitness. But in contrast to earlier times, the selection of sports and events for sponsorship was not so much based on patronage or local links but on raising awareness of products and building brand images. Although based on modern techniques of market research, the patterns of sponsorship matched the patterns of drink consumption which had existed since the turn of the century. Thus wines and spirits sponsorship was focused, in England at least, on those sports seen as being middle class, while brewers tended in the main to concentrate on mass spectator sports identified with the working class. Through its extensive financial backing of golf competitions in the 1960s and 1970s and particularly by its sponsorship of various Formula One racing teams, Martini positioned itself as an aspirational drink for the affluent classes which dovetailed perfectly with its TV evocations of sophisticated high living. Champagne producers concentrated on sports such as polo, yachting and equestrian events: Moet et Chandon no doubt hoped to establish drinking habits early through its sponsorship of public school cricket. In 1969 Bollinger opened their first tent at the British Open Golf Championship, establishing a 'tradition' that has grown to become a major attraction for well-heeled golf fans. For many years until 1982 Haig sponsored the National Village Cricket Championship, associating its whisky with the pastoral idyll of English cricket mythology as had been done by its rivals in the 1930s.[60]

Indeed, despite cricket's patrician image, its parlous financial state in the 1960s meant that it was one of the first sports to wholeheartedly embrace sponsorship. Much to the disgust of temperance reformers, when the 1969 MCC tourists left for Pakistan and Sri Lanka they were photographed on the steps of their aeroplane each holding a Cutty Sark Whisky carrier bag. The first sponsorship of a Test series took place the following year when the cancellation of the South African tour of England led to a hastily organised series against a Rest of the World side. The sponsorship of the series was originally offered to Harp by the cricket authorities but they failed to take it up and Guinness stepped in to take over the sponsorship at a cost of £40,000. Although the company had a long history of supporting cricket, its motivation was strictly commercial: 'it was a heaven sent opportunity to further the new image for Guinness which had been brought about by the outstanding success of Draught Guinness,' said their director of corporate affairs and sales.[61] From 1977 the county championship was sponsored by Schweppes, who despite not producing alcoholic drinks themselves were, in their role as a provider of soft-drinks mixers for spirits, quite definitely part of the trade, and long-term sponsorships of the English national side were arranged with Tetley's and subsequently with HP Bulmer's 'Scrumpy Jack' cider. Perhaps most notorious, from many cricket fans' point of view, was the agreement between Surrey and an Australian brewer which resulted in the Oval being renamed the Foster's Oval in honour of the self-proclaimed 'amber nectar'. A similar, albeit short-lived, deal saw the Headingley cricket and rugby league ground dubbed 'Bass Headingley' in the early 1990s.

Although rugby league had been quick to identify the opportunities available from sponsors in the early 1960s, football had been reluctant to become directly involved with the drinks sponsorship, partly because it didn't feel the financial necessity to do so but also because of residual doubts as to the respectability of advertising drink – a hesitation which continues today: in 1998 the FA deliberately deliberately excluded drinks companies from its list of preferred sponsors for the England team and the FA Cup.[62] However, the financial rewards available from sponsors and the growing acceptability of alcohol advertising both through television and the involvement of prominent players led in 1970 to the introduction of the Watney Cup knockout competition for Football League teams. In exchange for the naming of the tournament, which also had the honour of being the first to use penalty shoot-outs to decide drawn matches, the brewer paid £82,000. Its importance to the sport was far greater than simply adding a few more matches to a crowded season: it marked the beginning of the modern age of football sponsorship. Scotland followed suit the following year with the Drybrough Cup, based on the same format. Relaxations on both sides of the border to the rules governing shirt advertising meant that by the 1980s clubs were signing sponsorship deals which saw the names of brewers and their products adorning team shirts.

The 1990s saw the wholesale rebranding of competitions to attract sponsors in both England and Scotland (most notably seen in the transformation of the

League Cup into, successively, the Milk Cup, the Littlewoods Cup and so on), yet a proposed deal which would have seen the FA Cup renamed the Foster's Cup fell through, partially due to commercial difficulties but also to a major outcry against the branding of possibly the world's most famous football trophy with the name of an alcoholic drink. Nevertheless, the formation of the FA Premier League in 1993 was accompanied by a sponsorship agreement with Bass to call the new league the Carling Premier League. The Carling deal marked the beginning of Bass's domination of the game, as the brewers extended their sponsorship across football to promote the names of its brands in major competitions, such as the Worthington (formerly the League) Cup and the Tennent's Scottish Cup. By 1998 the company was spending over one million pounds per month sponsoring the Premier League alone.[63] Indeed, such was the popularity of football in the 1990s and the eagerness of brewers to be associated with it that new categories of sponsorship were dreamt up to provide brewers with something at which they could throw their money. Carlsberg, who had sponsored Liverpool since 1992, became the 'official beer' of the FA Cup, the European Cup Winners' Cup, the UEFA Cup and of the England team in the 1998 World Cup. Although this was an entirely vacuous form of sponsorship – one could have claimed with equal justification and considerably less outlay to be the 'unofficial beer' of these competitions – it did allow the company to use the official logos on their packaging and undertake a huge wave of identikit promotional activities in pubs.

The heightened importance of marketing and sponsorship to the breweries was further increased by another round of consolidation in the 1970s as brewers merged with other businesses in the leisure and food industries to form conglomerates – in 1972 Courage was taken over by Imperial Tobacco and in 1978 Allied took over J. Lyons & Co. The quickening pace of centralisation also meant that pubs were transformed increasingly into retail outlets of brewery chains. Although this process had been underway in varying degrees since the wholesale tying of pubs in the last decades of the nineteenth century, it was accelerated by the mergers and rebrandings of breweries and pubs in the 1960s and 1970s which took away much of the independence of the pub landlord. Thus it was the breweries, rather than the pubs themselves, which initiated the revival of traditional pub games in the 1970s and 1980s. Inspired somewhat by the success of televised darts and snooker – and by Yorkshire TV's weekly 'Indoor League' programme which featured pub games like arm-wrestling, skittles and dominoes – the attempt to reintroduce old games was based both on the need to attract more custom into their pubs and also to recreate the commonly-used marketing image of the timeless virtues of the typical British pub. Watney's played a major role in the continuing success story of darts in the 1970s, sponsoring the British Open Championship.[64]

After a long decline in the 1950s and 1960s which had seen many pubs dispose of their bowling greens, bowls also underwent a revival in the 1970s as breweries, particularly Tetley's and Mitchells and Butlers, sponsored both national and local competitions. Cobbold's brewery in Ipswich and Vaux in Sunderland had sponsored local quoits leagues since the late 1950s, and the 1970s saw Courage and Scottish and Newcastle breweries also begin sponsorship of the game, the latter promoting the first world championship since 1913.[65] In 1988 Samuel Webster and Wilsons sponsored the revival of 'log-end darts' in the North-West and in 1991 the Halifax-based Webster's Brewery sought to breathe life into knur and spell. In 1989 Scottish and Newcastle even sponsored a maggot-racing competition. Similarly, the traditions of football too were drawn upon by the marketeers in the 1990s when, as part of its promotional drive to reach soccer supporters, Carlsberg began the Carlsberg Pub Cup, open to all pub football teams which sold their lager.[66]

Although in England it was broadly true to say that brewers aimed the bulk of their sponsorship activities at sports seen as working class while distillers and wine merchants concentrated on middle-class sports, there were prominent exceptions. In 1979 Whitbread began to use the Queen's Club pre-Wimbledon tennis tournament in West London to ally the 'reassuringly expensive' brand values of Stella Artois with the leisure activities of the well heeled. Rugby union, with its deeply-ingrained culture of copious beer drinking, was an obvious target for brewery sponsorship as the sport's traditional objections to professionalism and commercialism began to fracture in the 1980s. As well as numerous club sponsorship deals – the earliest possibly being Whitbread's sponsorship of Askeans in the early 1980s – brewers played a key role in the sport's developing national profile. In 1994 Courage began sponsorship of rugby union's new league structure of ninety-five separate divisions, comprising over 1,200 clubs, as well as the England national side. Heineken, another Whitbread brand, which in the 1970s had used Scottish footballer Joe Jordan in its famous 'Heineken refreshes the parts others cannot reach' campaign, sponsored rugby union's World and European cups and tennis and yachting events to broaden its customer base. As rugby union turned professional in 1995, sponsors began to develop deep-going campaigns, which not only involved shirt sponsorship but also sought to support clubs at the local and junior levels. Tetley's national sponsorship of the game from 1998 actively sought to develop their links with clubs, providing free playing kit, post-protectors and balls, as well as advice on developing trade in club bars – the commercial benefits to the brewer being obvious.[67]

However, in Scotland the lines between drinking patterns were not as fixed and the greater consumption of spirits, especially whisky, among all sections of the population meant a far greater involvement of distillers in football. Most notable was Bell's £8 million sponsorship of the Scottish League Championship between 1994 and 1998. Drybrough's were not only the first company to sponsor a Scottish football competition but its marketing activities even took them south of the border as sponsors of the semi-professional Northern League in the early 1980s. Conversely, brewers appear to have been keener to sponsor non-football sports too, McEwans regularly sponsoring Scottish golf tournaments from the mid-1970s, perhaps in recognition of the broader social appeal of golf in Scotland. The distillers also provided powerful backing for traditional Scottish sports. As early as 1959 the Scotch Whisky Association had sponsored curling's first world championship, the winners of which received, perhaps unsurprisingly, the Scotch Whisky Cup. Shinty too benefited from the distillers, with Macdonald & Muir, through their most famous brand Glenmorangie, sponsoring the Camanachd Cup and other competitions from 1977, and Lang Brothers supporting the sport's oldest competition, the Glasgow Celtic Society Cup. By 1997 over 53 per cent of the sponsorship expenditure of Scottish distillers went to sport, compared to 33 per cent and 13 per cent to the arts and community projects.[68]

How successful was the drinks industry in turning its investment in sport into business advantage? The success of sponsorship is difficult to quantify and companies rarely comment other than favourably on such activities, but its growth and ubiquity would suggest that few companies believe that their involvement fails to meet their objectives. In 1982 the market research agency Sportscan could list ninety-two televised sporting events in Britain which were sponsored by drinks companies, to say nothing of those competitions which didn't appear on television. By 1988 sports sponsorship and associated activities accounted for over a quarter of the drinks industry's aggregate advertising budget of £158 million.[69] A tightening in the regulations relating particularly to lager advertisements in 1988 may have resulted in a shift from advertising to sponsorship – it is noticeable that in football many brand sponsorships are lager related. In 1998 Bass reported that during its sponsorship of football sales of its Carling lager rose by 31 per cent to become the UK's top-selling alcoholic brand. In 1999 the lager became the first drink in Britain to sell one billion pints in a single year. During England's Euro '96 campaign, sales of Carling rose by 72 per cent. In their period as 'official beer of the England team' for the 1998 World Cup Carlsberg saw its sales rise to three million pints in pubs and 45 million cans through off-licences. In Scotland, the period of Bells' football sponsorship saw their brand awareness – the measure of public recognition for the product – rise to 67 per cent, the highest for any brand of spirits in the UK Cider consumption trebled between 1960 and 1985, a direct consequence of the extensive advertising and sponsorship campaigns undertaken by the cider manufacturers, which focused especially on cricket and rugby union.[70] Certainly these achievements are in line with the apparent success of sports sponsorship in the United States, where Anheuser-Busch saw annual sales of their beers rise from under 6m barrels to over 35m during their 25-year involvement with sports.[71] However, to what extent such rises in sales are directly attributable to sponsorship is difficult to quantify; for example, major football tournaments will almost inevitably bring higher sales of alcohol as beer is bought to drink while watching matches whether at home or in a pub. Certainly, the influence of advertising on sales of alcohol appears to have a marginal effect in comparison to price and income factors – between 1975 and 1989 expenditure on alcohol advertising increased by almost 100 per cent, yet consumption rose only by around 7.5 per cent in the same period.[72]

Although increased sales and brand recognition represent the 'hard' returns on their investment, sponsorship also brought numerous 'soft', less tangible, benefits to drinks companies. Part of the appeal of sports sponsorship was that it allowed the drinks manufacturer to reap the benefits of a close identification with a club or sport without any of the attendant risks associated with holding shares or other financial commitments in a club. From the 1950s, the relationship of the drinks trade to football clubs in particular had changed from being one of direct support at board level to having an arms-length, albeit still mutually-beneficial, link. Vamplew's analysis of 39 English sports companies in 1901 showed that 11.6 per cent, or 27 out of 232, directors were linked with the drinks trade. By 1999 the percentage had dropped to just 4.8 per cent, or 11 out of 230, of which 3 were directors of wine merchants, 3 directors of hotels and 5 connected with the brewery trade.[73] Even a brewer such as J.W. Lees, which continued to hold a controlling interest in Oldham Athletic, saw themselves simply as a protective backstop and refused to provide money for the club to buy players in the late 1990s, preferring instead to reassure the club's supporters that 'whenever the club has been in a position where it needed financial support from J.W. Lees to secure its survival, J.W. Lees has always answered the call and provided it'.[74]

Sponsorship allowed companies to develop their business in other ways too. Sports events are ideal locations for wooing potential customers and extending relationships with existing clients, especially if the event carries the cachet of exclusivity or great popularity. The tremendous growth in the number of corporate boxes at all sports stadia since the early 1980s is testimony to this particular mix of business and pleasure. Many sponsorship deals also include benefits for the sponsor's staff, enabling them to get low-cost admission or merchandise, helping to cement feelings of loyalty to their employers. This inter-relationship between sport and the drinks industry is especially illuminated by the identification of a brand or company with a nationally-prominent sport or team, which also helps to increase the self-confidence of the sponsors and their marketing activities, especially when it is successful: as Bass's marketing department put it, 'When football succeeds, so does the brand.'[75] Shorn of its late-twentieth-century marketing jargon, the sentiment is no different from that of the brewers and distillers in Victorian times, whose financial and material support helped to establish and nurture their local clubs, and in many cases helped to protect them from the precarious economics of professional sport.

Notes

1. Peter Mathias, *The Brewing Industry in England, 1770–1830*, Cambridge, 1959; Kevin Hawkins, 'The Conduct and Development of the Brewing Industry in England and Wales 1880–1938', unpublished PhD thesis, University of Bradford, 1981; Brian Berrison and James P. Merrington, *The Centenary History of the Newcastle Breweries Ltd, 1890–1990*, Dunfermline, 1990, p. 59.

2. See Sidney Neville, *Seventy Rolling Years*, London, 1958, p. 90 and p. 199; Berry Ritchie, *An Uncommon Brewer*, London, 1992, p. 110.

3. For the Courage logo, see Mass-Observation Archive, File Report FR 3174, 'A Report on Courage Showcards', October 1949. For the story of Tetley's logo, see John Chartres, 'Joshua Tetley & Son, 1890s to 1990s' in John Chartres and Katrina Honeyman (eds), *Leeds City Business*, Leeds, 1993.

4. *The Licensing World*, 4 August, 1900 and 18 August 1900.

5. Tetley Archives, Box 58, Private Letter Books of C.F. Tetley, held by West Yorkshire Archive Service, Leeds.

6. Terry Gourvish, *Norfolk Beers from English Barley. A History of Steward & Patterson 1793–1963*, Norwich, 1987.

7. Ian Clarke, 'The Origins and Development of Cricket in Cornwall until 1900', unpublished MA dissertation, De Montfort University, 2000, p. 64.

8. Brian Glover, *Prince of Ales. The History of Brewing in Wales*, Stroud, 1993, p. 100 and p. 125; Tim Auty, John Jenkins and Duncan Pierce, *Who's Who of Welsh International Rugby Players*, Wrexham, 1991.

9. For more on the Beamish family see Peter Bills, *Passion in Exile. 100 Years of London Irish RFC*, Edinburgh 1998, p. 34.

10. Henry Mitchell & Co. Ltd., Managing Directors' Board Minutes, 21 June 1888.

11. *The Deerstalker*, vol. 1, no. 1, October 1948, p. 25.

12. Details taken from 'The Brewery Cricket Club' manuscript, dated 1900, in Tetley's Brewery Wharf Archive, Leeds.

13. *The Deerstalker*, vol. 1 no. 1, October 1948, p. 28.

14. Mitchells and Butlers, *Fifty Years of Brewing 1879–1929*, Birmingham, 1929, p. 101; *Athletic News*, 28 October 1889.

15. Mitchells and Butlers, *Fifty Years of Brewing 1879–1929*, p. 101.

16. *The Anchor*, August 1922, p. 99.

17. Hurford Janes, *The Red Barrel: A History of Watney Mann*, London, 1963, p. 183.

18. Truman's Board of Directors, Minutes of Meetings, 1 March 1923, Courage Brewery Archives, TA/C/1-31.

19. *Sports Dispatch*, 30 April 1927.

20. Consultative Committee Minutes, 18 August 1930, in Tetley's Brewery Wharf Archive, Leeds.

21. Geoffrey Channon, 'George's and Brewing in Bristol' in *Studies in the Business History of Bristol*, Bristol, 1988, p. 172.

22. H. & G. Simonds, Board of Directors, Minutes of Meetings, 22 March and 30 August 1937.

23. Worthington's Board of Directors, Minutes of Meetings, 13 November 1923, passim.

24. Worthington's Board of Directors, Minutes of Meetings, 7 May 1934 and 6 May 1940.

25. Simond's Board of Directors, Minutes of Meetings, 4 July 1960.

26. John Chartres, 'Joshua Tetley & Son, 1890s to 1990s', p. 114.

27. Scottish Brewers Ltd, Advertising Committee Minutes, 7 April 1932; John Arlott, *Krug. House of Champagne*, London, 1976, p. 124.

28 *The Oxford English Dictionary* (Second Edition, CD-Rom, 1992) records the first use of the term in England as being in 1928.

29. Henry Mitchell & Co. Ltd., Managing Directors' Board Minutes, 12 August 1907 and 17 August 1921. See also Matthew Taylor, '"Proud Preston": A History of the Football League', unpublished PhD thesis, De Montfort University, 1997, p. 45.

30. For Hearts see William Younger Directors' Minutes Books, 25 April 1905. For Wolves, see Inglis, *The Football Grounds of Great Britain*, London, 1987, p. 196. Wolves bought the ground from the brewery in 1923. For Oldham, see Graham Williams, *The Code War*, Harefield, 1994, p. 167.

31. For both Liverpool and Manchester United, see Inglis, *The Football Grounds of Great Britain*, p. 57 and p. 209; Taylor, 'Proud Preston', p. 45; Stephen Tischler, *Footballers and Businessmen*, New York, 1981, pp. 74–8.

32. Inglis, *The Football Grounds of Great Britain*, p. 228.

33. Simonds Board of Directors Minute Books 1922–1939, passim.

34. For Lloyd George, see *The Times*, 1 March 1915; Geoffrey Channon, 'George's and Brewing in Bristol' in *Studies in the Business History of Bristol*, p. 180.

35. Jim Davies, *The Book of Guinness Advertising*, London, 1998, pp. 7–39. See also F.G. Wigglesworth, 'The Evolution of Guinness Advertising', *Journal of Advertising*

History, 3 (March 1980); *The Cricketer*, 3 September 1955. Almost every other drink on the market claimed healthy credentials – including Bovril, milk, tea and Coca Cola – regardless of medical opinion; see John Burnett, *Liquid Pleasures: A Social History of Drinks in Modern Britain*, London, 1999.

36. Mass-Observation, *Report on Juvenile Drinking*, Sheffield, 1943, pp. 38–9.

37. For more on the background to the campaign see Mike Ripley and Fiona Wood, *'Beer is Best' The Collective Advertising of Beer 1933–1970*, London, 1994 and Sidney Neville, *Seventy Rolling Years*, pp. 222–3.

38. Statistics from Ripley and Wood, *'Beer is Best'* p. 16, and J. Baxter, 'The Organisation of the Brewing Industry', unpublished PhD, University of London, 1945, p. 267.

39. *Golf Illustrated*, 4 June 1938, p. 186.

40. For the background to the introduction of Red Barrel see Hurford Janes, *The Red Barrel: A History of Watney Mann*, London, 1963, p. 163 and Peter Haydon, *The English Pub*, London, 1994, p. 305. As Haydon points out, however, it was Flowers, rather than Watney's, who were the keenest to sell keg beer initially.

41. *The Cricketer Annual*, London, 1935, p. 39; *The Cricketer Spring Annual*, London, 1938, p. 39.

42. *Report of the Royal Commission on Licensing (England and Wales) 1929–1931*, London, 1932, p. 1214.

43. *The Cricketer Annual*, London, 1939, p. 69. *The Cricketer Spring Annual*, London, 1938, p. 49.

44. Wilson, *Alcohol and the Nation*, pp. 141–3.

45. *Report of the Royal Commission on Licensing (England and Wales) 1929–1931*, London, 1932, p. 106.

46. Truman's Board of Directors meeting minutes, passim. Details of the dispute with Ilford Golf Club can be found in the minutes of the 23 May 1935 meeting. (Courage Archives TA/C/1-31)

47. Bass Board of Directors meeting 9 November 1934.

48. Batley RUFC committee minutes, 1, 13 and 22 August 1935. Kirklees Archives, KC141.

49. Simonds Board of Directors Minute Books, 12 September 1927.

50. Simonds Board of Directors Minute Books, 26 March 1923 and 19 January 1948.

51. T.R. Gourvish and R.G. Wilson, *The British Brewing Industry*, Cambridge, 1994, p. 448.

52. See Leslie Dunkling and Gordon Wright, *A Dictionary of Pub Names*, London, 1987; Haydon, *The English Pub*, p. 312; *Roundabout* (Bass Worthington staff magazine), vol. 1 no. 3, (1974) p. 6.

53. Janes, *The Red Barrel*, p. 194; Ripley and Wood, *Beer is Best*, p. 12.

54. Mitchells and Butlers, Board of Directors' Meetings Minute Books, 16 July and 12 August 1906.

55. *Darts Weekly News*, 15 June 1937, 28 August, 1937 and 6 November 1937; *Score-Board*, 20 October 1948.

56. *Darts Weekly News*, 2 October 1937

57. Simonds Board of Directors Minute Books, September 1947.

58. Tennent Caledonian staff magazine, *The News*, June 1974.

59. Truman's Board of Directors meeting minutes, 1 June 1961; A.N Gaulton, *The Encyclopedia of Rugby League Football*, London, 1968, p. 89.

60. Francis Murray, *The Open*, London, 2000, p. 111; Derek Birley, *A Social History of English Cricket*, London, 1999, p. 307.

61. G.P. Williams and G.T. Brake, *Drink in Great Britain, 1900–1979*, London, 1979; Edward Guinness, *The Guinness Book of Guinness*, London, 1988, p. 442.

62. *Guardian*, 30 January 1988.

63. Bass Brewers, *Sponsorship: Mixing Business With Pleasure*, Burton, 1998, p. 2.

64. *The Times*, 30 December 1974; *Morning Advertiser*, 3 January 1975.

65. *Ipswich Evening Star*, 25 November 1957; *Morning Advertiser*, 25 May 1965; *Bristol Evening Post*, 6 March 1973; *Northern Echo*, 26 April 1986.

66. For an overview of the revival of pub games see Arthur Taylor, *The Guinness Book of Traditional Pub Games*, London, 1992.

67. Peter Mayle, *Thirsty Work – Ten Years of Heineken Advertising*, London, 1983. For more on Tetley's and Thwaites' sponsorship of rugby see *Running Rugby*, May/June 2000, pp. 20–3.

68. The authors are grateful to Dr Hugh Dan MacLennan for this information.

69. Sportscan (Sports Sponsorship Computer Analysis Ltd), *Analysis of Televised Sponsored Sport*, London, 1982; Tony Humphris, *Regulation of Alcohol Advertising and Sports Sponsorship in the U.K.* paper presented to the I.C.A.A. Conference, Stockholm, June 1991.

70. Burnett, *Liquid Pleasures*, p. 158.

71. Bass Brewers, *Sponsorship*, p. 4; Anon, *Superbrands*, London, 1998, pp. 24–5 and pp. 34–5; Robert Stainback, *Alcohol and Sport*, Champaign, Illinois, 1997 pp. 27–8.

72. Christine Godfrey, *Preventing Alcohol and Tobacco Problems*, vol. 1, London, 1990.

73. Wray Vamplew, *Pay Up and Play the Game*, Cambridge, 1988, p. 168. Current data from Annual Returns to Companies House made by the clubs between 1996 and 1999.

74. J.W. Lees, statement in Oldham Athletic match day programme 14 November 1998, p. 3.

75. Bass Brewers, *Sponsorship*, p. 4.

3

Cheers! Alcohol and the Sporting Crowd

It is no exaggeration to suggest that, no matter what the sport or its level of popularity, the consumption of alcohol is almost an intrinsic part of the spectator experience. Indeed, it would be difficult to argue with the contention that for many spectators, the activity on the field of play is often secondary to the opportunity to drink: few advertising slogans have expressed a greater truth than Double Diamond's 1960's catchphrase 'I'm only here for the beer'.

In pre-industrial times when sporting activity took place as a part of fairs, festivals and holidays and the division between participant and observer was not always clear, sport and the drinking of alcohol were closely intertwined parts of the same experience. Whether it was the drinking booths at horse racing, the inns which staged cockfighting or the individual beer-sellers who lined the routes to major sporting events, attendance at a sports event was accompanied by almost limitless opportunities to imbibe. The traditional hostility of the temperance movement to sport, at least until the final quarter of the nineteenth century, was based largely on the fact that where there was sport, there was alcohol – with, so they believed, licentiousness, immorality and despair inevitably following.

Certainly at the larger horse-racing events, drunken revelry was a constant source of concern for the authorities and a vital part of the sport's appeal to not inconsiderable sections of its crowd. Sport during festivals and holidays was part of the process of release from the rigours of winter, the toil of the summer or demands of the harvest. It was a time for the relaxing of inhibitions and cultivation of indulgence. And it was this sense of the complementary relationship of alcohol and sport in a rural environment which meant that drink was an inextricably interwoven strand in the fabric of the sporting experience.

Not surprisingly, this tradition of drinking while watching sport continues strongly in those sports connected with the rural past. Alcohol was, and continues to be today, a vital ingredient of hunting and shooting. The hip flask was as much a part of the hunter's and the shooter's equipment as stirrups or spare cartridges, acting as a stimulant, protection against the cold and a social lubricant as it was passed around friends. Although whisky tended to be a regular in the hip flask, the more imaginative sportsman or woman may have chosen gin, schnapps or a home-made concoction. The ritual of the hunt invariably began with communal imbibing, whether of punch, port or whisky. Even if the hunters felt disinclined to share their drink with onlookers, the fact that the hunt would often meet at a local pub before going in pursuit of its prey meant that spectators would not be lacking in alcoholic fortification.[1]

At a more plebeian level, the popularity of drinking among horse-racing spectators began to be perceived as a problem in the mid-nineteenth century by the horse-racing authorities, who from the 1870s sought to curb many of the more unruly aspects of race meetings by stricter regulation of both gambling and drinking. Although crowd disorder was usually ascribed to spectator dissatisfaction with welshing bookmakers or jockeys who appeared not to be trying, alcohol was often felt to inflame such situations further. These moves to restrict alcohol consumption may have also been facilitated by the fact that rental income from drinking booths was declining in importance to promoters as gate money began to be charged. Anti-gambling campaigners would also attempt to stop the granting of drink licences by local magistrates to prevent meetings going ahead or to restrict the appeal of racing. Often magistrates needed no prompting to undermine the attraction of drinking at the races; in 1908 the appeal of going to Chesterfield racecourse was radically reduced when local magistrates halved the opening hours for on-course drinking booths from noon until 10 p.m. to a more decorous 1 p.m. until 6 p.m. The modernisation of racing from the mid-nineteenth century onwards – through the advent of the railways, the building of enclosed racecourses, and the creation of a national racing structure – changed the spectating experience from being akin to attending a fair or festival to being a consumer of a controlled, time-limited event, thus reducing, but not removing, the opportunities for alcoholic over-indulgence. Nevertheless, even today a large measure of the appeal of a race meeting is the proliferation of bars at courses and the ability to drink at length throughout the day – so much so that in 1999 Uttoxeter racecourse generated 25 per cent of its race-day takings through bar sales and Cheltenham estimated that their annual bar turnover was around £500,000.[2]

Much of the pre-industrial idea of the sporting event being an occasion for drinking was carried over into modern football. 'Going to the Match' became an experience in itself, encompassing the journey to and from the game, the playing of the game, the meeting of friends and acquaintances, eating and, of course, the consumption of beer, particularly immediately before, during, and, at greater length, after the match. The fact that football matches were more than simply a time for viewing sporting endeavour but were also an occasion for drinking did not go unnoticed by temperance campaigners. In 1908 C.T. Studd, the Christian sports enthusiast, bemoaned the fact that:

a man cannot attend even a football match without making his way to the refreshment bar. It is at the part nearest the drinking bar that one hears the worst language. Men frequently get half-intoxicated and, in most cases, bad-tempered, and so the good name of sport is taken away, never to return until the drinking booths are abolished . . . let us look with shame upon the intoxicant, and ask the managers and committees of clubs to order the instant closing of refreshment bars.[3]

Needless to say, in most cases this was a forlorn hope; and not simply because of the financial implications to any club which closed its bars to supporters. To do so would have undermined much of the appeal of going to a football match. Indeed, many middle-class commentators on the nature of the football crowd felt that watching sport was morally inferior to playing it and would have preferred the working classes not to have gone to watch professionals play football. Writers such as Studd failed to understand the collective pleasures and the attendant emotions which were kindled by going to a match. And drink played a central role in that experience. Nor was the importance of alcohol to the experience of travelling to a sporting event confined to football – during Henley week in 1900 *Licensing World* helpfully printed photographs of all those 'noted riverside hostelries' along the Thames which spectators would pass on their way to the event.[4] In contrast to worries of the teetotallers, the attraction of drink to the football supporter, and in particular the drinking of the relatively new bottled beer, was somewhat lyrically described by a contributor to *The Licensed Victualler* in 1900 in his description of a Tottenham Hotspur crowd:

here and there protruded the ominous neck of a bottle, which told of the forethought of some in preparing for emergencies, in the shape of the resuscitation of the vocal strings, which a lengthy period of rest had somewhat impaired. O weary men! Chips off the old block! Who can tell how many greedy eyes were transfixed as the 'elixir of youth' was raised to quench the parched throat?[5]

The common use of bottled beer at matches by supporters is also attested to by many contemporary photographs of crowds at or on the way to matches. In 1910 Swindon newspapers noted that 'suspicious black bottles' were being passed around the crowd at Swindon Town's County Ground.[6] Trips to London from the north for the FA Cup Final especially were occasions for copious indulgence. When Bradford City won the Cup at Crystal Palace in

1911, local newspapers reported that numerous crates of beer accompanied City supporters on their journey to the capital, with some fans getting so drunk on the journey that they were unable to attend the match.[7] This was a pattern which would repeat itself for the next sixty or seventy years, as supporters travelling to London for the FA Cup or Rugby League Challenge Cup finals used the travelling time to maximise their drinking opportunities. And, of course, in many instances the trips to cup finals – or in Scotland the 'brake clubs' through which supporters saved the money to travel to big games – were organised by and started from pubs.

The growth of supporters' clubs from the 1920s was also accompanied by the involvement of breweries in financing the provision of a bar for many such clubs. Both Truman's and Simonds were loaning money to Tottenham Hotspur Supporters' Club from the early 1930s, a pattern which was to be regularly repeated around the country throughout the following decades.[8] The value to a brewery of the business generated by a supporters' club can be gauged by the fact that in 1956 Truman's felt sufficiently confident in the drinking capacities of football fans to loan £1,500 to non-league Rainham FC's supporters' club, repayable over five years.

Income from supporters' clubs and bars inside the ground could make a substantial contribution to a club's financial health. In the late 1960s, both Coventry and Manchester City built new social clubs in order to capitalise on their supporters' complementary love of alcohol and their teams. Manchester City's cost £100,000 to build but by 1971 it was clearing an annual profit of £14,000 as supporters flocked to share a drink and occasionally rub shoulders with City players.[9] By 1984, a Department of the Environment working group noted that bar profits for some leading clubs totalled more than £100,000 per season, with the more marketing-aware clubs such as Rangers and Manchester United seeking to lever even more profit from supporters through the introduction of lager and whisky branded with the club's colours and name.[10]

The importance of the pub to the match-going experience was highlighted by a Mass-Observation investigator in 1948 who visited The Holte pub next to Aston Villa's ground on a Saturday afternoon. He noted with surprise that shortly before the pre-match rush began at 1.45 p.m. the pub's landlord stopped serving best beer, in order not to run out of supplies for regular customers during the rest of the week, and untruthfully told customers that he had run out and only had less alcoholic and cheaper beer for sale. 'A very large number' of customers also drank their beer from half-pint glasses, suggesting that getting drunk before the match was not their aim, despite the fact that, as the M-O investigator pointed out, Villa Park at this time did not have any licensed bars in the ground. The fact that the pub was part of the social routine of match-going was highlighted by the fact that many people used the pub to meet other supporters before going to the match and to eat lunch, rolls and sandwiches being a popular accompaniment to beer. Although customers came into the pub in waves, presumably dictated by the rhythm of public transport, the peak time for the pub lasted only half an hour, ending around 2.15 p.m., as customers left to join the queues to get into Villa Park.[11]

But beer was more than simply an accompaniment to football; in many cases it was part of the way in which supporters used sport as a means of asserting their identity. The fact that, until the late 1950s at least, many of the brewers who advertised in match-day programmes or whose name was painted across the roof of a stand were local companies, was an element of the civic pride and local identity which underpinned the appeal of football. Loyalty to a local beer was often as strong as loyalty to the local team – for many men defining their identity through their team, their local pub and their local beer was often as important as their political, religious and social affiliations.[12] Local and national identities were factors which were not ignored by breweries when marketing their beer: in the 1930s Norwich's Steward & Paterson's advertising slogan was 'Buy British . . . and help your County, your Country and your Empire'.[13] It is perhaps unsurprising therefore that the local outcry which greeted the takeover of Barnsley Brewery by John Smiths in the 1960s was explained by the historian of the Courage group in football terms: 'There has always been a strong local feeling for Barnsley Bitter, an emotional loyalty which is as keenly expressed as that for Barnsley FC whose ground adjoins the brewery.'[14] At a regional level too, the widespread assumption among northern English sports fans that beer in the south of England is flatter, weaker and generally less palatable than beer in the north is held to be symbolic of a softer, less competitive way of playing football, cricket and rugby. And this in turn highlights the fact that it is not only geographical identity which joins together local beer and football – the two are also tightly bound together as part of what it means to be a man. The ability to consume large amounts of beer, or to be able to 'hold your ale' is an important test of masculinity among large sections of males of all classes. Nowhere has this been more graphically highlighted than in the terrace songs and chants of young male football supporters. Out of many, a variation on 'All the Nice Girls Love A Sailor', sung since the 1970s by supporters of Sheffield United (nicknamed the Blades), neatly, if distastefully, encapsulates the triumvirate of football, beer and manhood:

> All the Blade Men love their gravy [beer]
> All the Blade Men love to spew
> 'Cos when you've had a triple gallon

It's the natural thing to do.
Nice and greasy, goes down easy
And it comes up just the same.
So if you see a fellow spew, it's the natural thing to do
Call him a Blademan – cos that's his name.

In other examples of the genre, Port Vale supporters claimed in their version of the Beatles' 'Yellow Submarine' to drink ten pints of beer before going to see their team while Liverpool fans' 1978 rendition of 'Lili Marlene' admitted that they were 'bevvied up of course'.[15]

The importance of the ritual of the after-match drink was illustrated by market research undertaken in the 1960s by the Brewers' Society, which found that a football match or race meeting was the fifth most-likely location from which to travel to a pub, with 2 per cent of all pub-goers interviewed having come from such an event. In contrast, those who were going to a sporting event from the pub made up less than 0.5 per cent of those interviewed. The preference for drinking after a match seems to have been a constant throughout the twentieth century – in 1900 *The Licensed Victualler* noted that, even for those with the time, 'on the outward journey, the temptations of the "half-way house" appealed to few' on their way to White Hart Lane. In the 1920s Liverpool magistrates forbade pubs in the vicinity of Anfield and Goodision from opening during or after matches in order to minimise the risk of after-match drinking resulting in violent behaviour on Saturday nights, although the efficacy of such measures is unclear.[16]

Club Culture and Middle-class Drinkers

However, it is perhaps in those sports which are perceived as being middle class in which the after-match drinking ritual is most developed. The culture of the '19th Hole' has become as much a part of the leisure golfer's experience as the sliced drive and the errant putt. As advertising in golf magazines demonstrated, the drink of choice of the golf enthusiast was more likely to be whisky or gin than beer but the importance of alcohol was hardly less. Many histories of local golf clubs devote considerable space to the development of the clubhouse – indeed, one of the proudest claims of a history of Tyneside Golf Club was that the club still held the first spirit measure it acquired, dating back to 1879.[17] The overt centrality of drinking to the culture of the golf club can be seen somewhat bizarrely in the justifications advanced for the anti-Semitic policies which excluded many Jews from golf clubs: even as late as 1975 a historian of golf in Britain could seriously argue that 'Jews do not indulge to any great extent in intoxicating liquors . . . since most golf clubs rely heavily on bar profits, there is a practical unwillingness to admit too many Jews.'[18]

Rugby union clubs shared many of the social characteristics of golf clubs, but in contrast beer tended to be the drink of choice in the clubhouse. Heavy drinking had always been a feature of varsity and medical school rugby, but it appears that the installation of bars into rugby union clubs from the 1920s helped to cement the strong role which after-match sociability played within rugby union as a whole. In contrast to soccer, after-match drinking in rugby generally took place between players and spectators, who were more often than not members of the club and probably former players themselves. It was this inclusiveness which was used by supporters of rugby union to demonstrate that, contrary to the opinion of many outside of the sport, their game was not a bastion of social exclusivity and snobbery. Many of these social clubs, such as that of London Irish, grew from being nothing more than a beer barrel on a trestle table in a tea room, from which the tradition of heavy drinking until long into the early hours of the following morning developed. More often than not, this was accompanied by the rendition of songs celebrating alleged feats of alcoholic and sexual indulgence, no less offensive than those sung on the terraces by football supporters but less public because done within the confines of a private club.

As with drinking and singing at football matches, the rituals of rugby drinking were closely associated with the proclamation of masculinity – beer, or perhaps cider in the south-west of England, was seen as the drink of a man with all others, save for whisky, being scorned as effeminate. The after-match 'session' with its emphasis on the number of pints which could be drunk, together with the subsequent tales of copious consumption, was a vital aspect of the rugby union experience. The club itself was a masculine republic, with women generally confined to serving beer or preparing food. Indeed, their presence as guests in the club was not generally welcomed either: talking about the 1950s and 1960s, one stalwart of London Irish noted that in the social club 'girlfriends were just regarded as being in the way'.[19]

Although the anti-social behaviour seen at football grounds rarely took place at a rugby union match, save for the occasional streaker or inebriate wandering onto the pitch, the fact that after-match antics sometimes paralleled too closely the behaviour of lower-class football louts did begin to cause concern for some in rugby union in the late 1960s and 1970s. Nevertheless, 'high jinks', as such behaviour was euphemistically known, were seen as an integral part of the appeal of being involved in rugby union by many of its adherents. The drunken antics of Harlequins touring parties was justified by a historian of the club in 1991 with the argument that:

hotels knew very well what might be in prospect when they booked in an entire Rugby football team and its administration, and adjusted their prices accordingly. Bar sales shot up to record heights, for the presence of the club in the hotel drew in large numbers of other drinkers, anxious to see these 'foreigners' at close quarters. Some of the escapades became legends and furnished a topic of bar conversation for years to come.[20]

No doubt the same arguments could be employed by any number of football hooligans too.

It was probably not coincidental that the one rugby union region which did take steps to curb spectator drinking and its associated activity was Wales, where rugby union had always encompassed both the middle and working classes. Drunken behaviour by young working-class Welsh males was viewed in different terms than that of a crowd of Oxbridge undergraduates at the Varsity Match – what was seen by the authorities as high spirits by the latter was generally interpreted as the precursor to more serious disorder when engaged in by those who had learned their rugby in the pit villages and steel towns of south Wales. In the 1970s Welsh rugby union began to experience something of an 'alcohol problem', with Cardiff police regularly reporting up to fifty arrests for drink-related offences at international matches. Far from treating the problem as inconsequential revelry, and fearful of being tarred with the same brush as soccer, the Welsh Rugby Union in 1980 banned alcohol from being brought into Cardiff Arms Park on match days, and police watched the turnstiles at the ground with orders to search anyone suspected of carrying drink.[21]

Such a course of action almost violated the spirit of international rugby union. The alcoholic diversion offered by the journey to and from a Five Nations match had long demonstrated the truth of the adage that it is 'better to travel than to arrive', especially if one's allegiance was to a losing team. The trains that left Cardiff and Swansea to go to Twickenham or Murrayfield were loaded up with beer crates by supporters 'like soldiers rushing ammunition to guns', as W. John Morgan described a Welsh excursion to Murrayfield in 1955.[22] Drinking and being drunk were as much a part of the experience as a thrilling Welsh backline move.

In a similar way, the Oxford-Cambridge Varsity Match has also been an occasion for concentrated indulgence over the decades. Although its relevance as a rugby match has declined hugely since the inter-war years, when it was regarded effectively as a trial match for the Five Nations, its importance as a social event has quite possibly increased since the mid-1980s. Whereas once it marked the coming of Christmas holidays for the tens of thousands of undergraduates who flocked to Twickenham, today it has become the unofficial start of the Christmas drinking season for those employed in the City and its allied professions. The importance of after-match drinking to the culture of rugby union can be gauged by the fact that after a major game such as an international or the Varsity Match, Twickenham would expect to sell in excess of 10,000 pints of beer. As one journalist observed following an England match in February 2000: 'The boos which greeted the announcement that "the bars will remain closed after the match" were the loudest noise the Twickenham crowd made all afternoon.'[23]

However, the coming of open professionalism into rugby union has begun to change the relationship of spectators to their team, as clubs transform themselves from being an associations of members to becoming professional sports organisations, undermining the traditional culture of the game. For example, at Leicester members complained that the advent of professionalism meant that they could no longer drink in certain bars or use the club restaurant when they wanted because these areas were being used for corporate hospitality events where, no doubt, the drinking was no less copious but geared to more definite business goals. However, in an attempt to boost attendances at Newcastle in 1999, the club's management harked back to the earlier traditions of the sport by offering free beer to spectators for an hour after their game against Gloucester.[24]

Other factors have also helped to restrict and undermine the traditional drinking cultures of middle-class, club-based sports. The introduction of drink-driving laws and the breathalyser test for motorists in 1967 meant that it was no longer possible to drink to excess at a rugby or golf club and then drive home without fear of being stopped by the police. The increasing concern about drinking and driving by society, often expressed through harrowing television commercials, has also meant that social disapproval has become a major disincentive to club-based drinking by drivers.[25]

Although cricket had much in common with the 'clubability' of golf and rugby union – and excessive indulgence in beer has long been a feature of many cricket clubs' annual dinners – the length and nature of the game meant that its spectators' relationship to drink differed somewhat.[26] Despite the fact that many late eighteenth- and early nineteenth-century grounds were built adjacent to pubs, there appears to be no evidence that drink was behind the crowd disorders which took place in cricket's pre-modern phase.[27] This may be due to the fact that contemporary commentators paid little attention to the relative sobriety of the crowd and that a certain level of intoxication was the norm during this period. However, it does seem to be the case that cricket crowds in the Victorian and Edwardian periods were generally less inclined to drink and gamble at matches than their forebears. Given the numbers that attended major matches, cricket appears to be relatively free from crowd disturbances. This was not because cricket grounds were islands of temperance: bars were open for members and non-members were perfectly at liberty to bring their own drink into grounds. It may have owed something to the fact that, unusually for the time, crowds were socially mixed, forcing the middle-class spectators to exercise self-control over themselves and social control over their fellow, albeit lower-class, spectators. It may also have been because drinking was slower and took place over a longer period, in contrast to football or rugby where there was more incentive to drink quickly before the match and at half-time. Indeed, the fact that generally one could drink all day without interruption at a cricket ground became a particularly attractive feature of the sport in the inter-war years, following the introduction of highly regulated pub opening hours during the First World War. One witness at the 1929 Royal Commission on Licensing noted that the Oval on match days was especially popular with businessmen seeking alcoholic refreshment outside of normal opening hours.[28]

Alcohol begins to loom larger in the game with the introduction of one-day cricket competitions and Sunday play in the 1960s. The path for these developments had been laid down in large part by the success of the Lord's Taverners in the 1950s, who toured the country playing charity matches on Sundays for the disabled and other causes; their very name suggesting the traditional pleasures of willow against leather in the shade of a country inn. The large crowds attracted to one-day cricket, and especially from 1968 following the inauguration of the John Player-sponsored Sunday League, not only brought a desperately needed boost to county coffers but also a different type of spectator, one less inclined to abide by cricketing decorum and more likely to want to shout, sing and drink ostentatiously at matches. Although impossible to quantify, it is generally accepted that one-day cricket saw an increase in drunkenness at matches and a rise in football-crowd-type behaviour. Depending on one's stance, the exuberance of Lancashire and Somerset supporters in particular, and especially at the finals of the Gillette or Benson and Hedges Cup at Lords, was either a short step away from hooliganism or the creation of a carnival atmosphere similar to cricket in the West Indies.

Such developments were not welcomed by the MCC or, subsequently, by the TCCB. So it was ostensibly to stop alcohol-inspired disorder that the English cricket authorities sought to curb the enthusiasm of supporters of the West Indies in the 1970s and 1980s, whose beer cans and steel pans accompanied their side's regular demolition of England sides, by banning the use of musical instruments and (empty) alcohol containers used as such. The impact of this was simply to deter West Indian cricket supporters from attending Test matches in large numbers, precisely at a time when the sport was in need of all the support it could muster. In fact, the chief source of crowd problems in the late 1980s and 1990s proved to be England supporters – drink was held to be the cause of problems both serious, such as the racist abuse of black and Asian players at Headingley Test matches, and trivial, including the curmudgeonly ban placed on spectators wearing fancy-dress costumes at Test matches at the same ground in 1997.

In 1998, following crowd disturbances at Edgbaston, Lancashire banned spectators bringing their own drink into Old Trafford for that year's Test match, although this ban did not apply to Lancashire county members. The managements of Trent Bridge and Headingley also stopped spectators with tickets to certain parts of their grounds bringing in alcohol to Test matches. In fact, it is probable that these bans on bringing drinks into the ground were a case of commercialism dressed up as social concern – it was estimated that an average spectator at a Test match drinks between three and a half and five pints of beer on each day of the game; those that brought their own beer were therefore making substantial inroads into the bar profits of Old Trafford. Doubts about the sincerity of the controls on alcohol were kindled by the fact that the bars in these grounds remained open throughout the day. As many journalists pointed out at the time, the instigators of the ban seemed oblivious either to the irony of the England team being sponsored by Tetley's Bitter or the hypocrisy involved in seeking to curb the drinking of those who paid to watch the game while doing everything in their power to allow those in the corporate hospitality boxes and tents to maximise their drinking opportunities.[29]

The growth of corporate hospitality was one of the most marked changes in British sport from the 1970s. Partly a result of the increasing levels of business sponsorship of sport and partly a recognition by sports clubs and organisations that significant amounts of money could be earned by providing exclusive drinking facilities for businessmen and their clients, hospitality boxes and tents came to cast an important shadow over all levels of the sporting landscape. In effect they gave rise to a new type of sports spectator: one who had no intrinsic interest in the sport or any emotional stake in the outcome of the contest. Indeed, at best they could be thought of as 'sports tourists', attending different sports events in the same way in which they attended holiday destinations, soaking up the atmosphere and then moving on. The only constants for such spectators were free admission, the free food and the free drink.

Unsurprisingly, this caused significant friction with committed supporters of sport: golf enthusiasts complained about corporate guests at the British Open who stayed in the free drink tents all day and never saw a ball hit; tennis fans protested at those who wandered in to the Centre Court at Wimbledon halfway through a match after finishing their extensive lunches; most of all, football supporters condemned the corporate hospitality boxes which sprang up on every ground and at many took up room on the terraces which had been home to supporters for decades. The importance of the corporate box to soccer clubs can be gauged by the fact that in 1985 Tottenham Hotspur received around £750,000 for the rental of their seventy-two corporate boxes but expected that to be cut to less than £200,000 if drinking while watching a football match was banned, as was proposed under the 1985 Sporting Events (Control of Alcohol etc.) Act. Spurs were not alone – Manchester United estimated that they lost over £500,000 in the first season that alcohol was banned from executive boxes and thirty-three other clubs reported significant losses to a 1986 Home Office Committee enquiry. Unsurprisingly, the 1986 Home Office Committee of Inquiry recommended that the ban on alcohol in executive, or corporate, boxes should be reviewed.[30]

Hooliganism and the Demonisation of Drink

The 1985 Act was in fact the culmination of almost two decades of debate about the influence of alcohol on sports spectators and particularly its relation-ship to the problem of football hooliganism. Although crowd disorder at soccer and rugby matches in the late-Victorian and Edwardian eras was not infrequent and continued sporadically during the inter-war years, 'football hooliganism' as a social problem only began to emerge in the late 1950s, becoming a matter for regular concern for the football authorities, law enforce-ment agencies and politicians by the mid-1960s. In the 1880s and 1890s, at the start of the football boom, a large body of opinion felt that the game's popularity actually helped to decrease drunkenness and its attendant evils. Complaints from publicans about low takings on Saturday afternoons were not uncommon. Giving evidence to the 1898 Royal Commission on the Liquor Licensing Laws, the Chief Constable of Liverpool felt that the success of the two soccer clubs had led to a decline in drunkenness in the city as men no longer went straight to the pub after leaving work early on Saturdays. The Report of the Commission went so far as to argue that 'the passion for games and athletics – such as football and bicycling – which has been so remarkably stimulated during the past quarter of a century, has served as a powerful rival to "boozing", which at one time was the only excitement open to working men'.[31] This belief that the fall in the rates of arrest for drunkenness which had been seen in the last twenty years of the nineteenth century could be attributed to the tremendous popularity of outdoor sport was widespread: Austen Chamberlain in his budget speech of 1905 expressed the commonly-held opinion that 'the mass of our people are beginning to find other ways of expending some portion of time and money which used previously to be spent in the public house. No change has been more remarkable in the habits of the people than the growing attendance in the last fifteen years at outdoor games and sports.'[32] The argument that sporting activity helped to reduce drunkenness was also used in the 1930s by opponents of local authority clampdowns on pub games in Glasgow; protesting that bans on darts, dominoes and other games in licensed premises would only increase binge drinking, they pointed to Liverpool where a similar ban existed and where the city had a rate of arrests for drunkenness which was 150 per cent higher than the national average.[33]

In England up to the mid-twentieth century, alcohol had rarely been seen as a cause of hooliganism – anti-alcohol commentators being more concerned with the moral effects of drink – and it is noticeable that the official reports into the overcrowding at the first Wembley Cup Final in 1923 and the 1946 Bolton crowd disaster when thirty-three people were killed did not mention alcohol at all. That alcohol consumption by supporters was generally not thought of as a problem can be seen in a handbill distributed to its supporters by Millwall in the late 1940s warning them about their behaviour, entitled 'Don't Do It Chums', which made no mention of drunkenness or alcohol.[34] A Mass-Observation investigator at Bolton Wanderers' Burnden Park for a match in the late 1930s noted, in a revealing turn of phrase, that 'during the interval the bars are crowded' but reported no signs of drunkenness or related misbehaviour. Nevertheless, there were exceptions and in 1949 Sheffield United stopped selling alcohol at Bramall Lane because of drink-related incidents.[35] Despite the claims of the 1990 Taylor Report into the Hillsborough crowd disaster, there is no evidence that drinking among football supporters increased during the 1950s and 1960s, but alcohol did become an easy and convenient peg on which to hang the blame for the tribal and xenophobic violence which became a feature not only of football but of British society as a whole from the late 1950s.

In Scotland, opinion was more mixed. In 1883 the *Scottish Athletic Journal* had noted that 'The football field is one of the strongest temperance agents existing, and during a popular match, the bars are almost entirely deserted. The working population must be amused – is it to be the football field or the dram shop?'[36] But especially from the 1890s, as arrests for drunkenness in Scotland, although declining in the decades before the First World War, continued to be higher than in England and Wales, football was held to be to blame for drawing young men into drinking and for inciting violent reactions among the crowds watching the game. However, this view may have had more to do with the prevalence of Presbyterian and teetotal traditions among law-enforcement agencies than with any real differences in the drinking habits of

of alcohol may be consumed throughout the week'. There was little to back this up and its relevance to drinking at football matches was somewhat tangential. The report further undermined its own case by pointing out that police found scant evidence of drunkenness among football spectators. This latter assertion was strengthened by the increasing realisation that organised groups of thugs, such as the more notorious gangs, or 'crews', of Chelsea, West Ham or Leeds United supporters, deliberately eschewed alcohol on match days in order to keep their wits keen and fighting skills sharp.[43]

However, alcohol made a convenient scapegoat and was simple to act against, and in July 1985 the Sporting Events (Control of Alcohol etc.) Act found its way onto the statute books. Aside from the ill-fated attempt to introduce identity cards for football supporters, this was the centrepiece of the Thatcher government's strategy to eradicate football hooliganism. Like the Scottish Criminal Justice Act of 1980, it made it illegal to drink, or allow to be drunk, or to possess alcohol on a coach or train going to a football match, but it also made it illegal to take drink into a match or to possess it where the match could be seen. Moreover, it was illegal to be drunk at a game or going into a ground (although, unlike road traffic legislation, it made no attempt to define 'drunk') or for clubs to sell alcohol during a game without a magistrate's order. Cans and bottles were banned from grounds. Somewhat incongruously, it also banned the possession of fireworks inside a ground as well, unless done 'with lawful authority'.

In fact, the word 'sport' in the title of the Act was a misnomer as the legislation was entirely directed at soccer and made no mention of any other sport whatsoever. The statutory instrument which selected the stadia and events covered by the act defined a sports ground as being that of any club affiliated to the English, Scottish or Welsh Football Associations or where international soccer took place. A sporting event was defined as involving at least one club which was a member of the English or Scottish Football Leagues or was involved in a UEFA or FIFA match. The absence of any attempt to restrict alcohol consumption at other sports, despite the heavy drinking which took place at them, actually undermined the argument which underpinned the Act: if alcohol was the cause of, or at least a major contributor to, violent behaviour why did the Act concern itself only with football?

The Act made no appreciable difference to the level of violence at football matches, which was more affected by the wholesale use of closed-circuit television systems inside and outside of grounds and the increasingly large police presences at matches. The 1986 Home Office Report into Crowd Safety reviewed the impact of the Act and, as well as recommending the lifting of the ban on alcohol in executive boxes, supported continuing the stringent controls on alcohol at matches. Confusingly, it also quoted from the report of the 1968 Working Party in support of allowing alcohol licences for football grounds.[44] The same uncertainty was demonstrated by the Taylor Report into the 1989 Hillsborough disaster, which recognised that hardcore hooliganism had little to do with drink but argued that it could cause others to act impulsively and that, therefore, the restrictions on the sale of alcohol at grounds should remain in force. It explicitly linked the rise in football hooliganism in the 1960s with the increased availability of alcohol:

> drinking before matches increased in parallel with the growth of the hooliganism. Before the five day week, those coming straight from work to the football ground had little time to drink excessively. During the 1960s and 1970s young men in their twenties acquired a new affluence and spending on drink increased. The advent of the supermarket with an off-licence provided numerous outlets for the sale of canned beer; so it became easy to have alcohol at the match and on the way to it, whether the local pubs were open or not.[45]

This is a seductive yet misleading analysis. Drunkenness at matches was not unknown before the general introduction of the five-day week, as contemporary reports and the 1899 and 1909 Scottish riots demonstrated. Spending on drink may have increased but beer consumption per head of the population, even at its height in the mid-1970s, was significantly lower than at any point in the thirty years before the First World War, when football established its hold over the male population. And, as we have seen, it has always been easy 'to have alcohol at the match and on the way to it'.[46]

But the report's analysis was undermined not simply by its misreading of history. None of the many academic studies of hooliganism carried out in the 1980s and early 1990s found any evidence to suggest that drink was an important factor in football violence. 'Drinking cannot be said to be a "deep" cause of football hooliganism for the simple reason that not every fan drinks,' argued Eric Dunning, Patrick Murphy and John Williams in their 1988 *The Roots of Football Hooliganism*.[47] And, as a number of commentators noted, the reverse was also true: not every fan who drank, even heavily, was a hooligan. In particular, Danish soccer supporters, known as 'Roligans' from the Danish word for peace, 'rolig', combined both prodigious drinking feats with an equally large reputation for good humour and non-violence. Some writers on the subject, such as Peter Marsh and Kate Fox Kilby in their 1992 *Drinking and Public Disorder* use these examples to argue that claims of drink-inspired football hooliganism are a form of 'moral panic' with little basis in fact.[48]

It wasn't even necessary to look at Europe for examples. Scotland supporters evolved from being the media's feared archetype of drunken marauding thugs – best exemplified in the tabloid imagination by their pitch invasion and subsequent dismantling of the Wembley goalposts following the Scots' 2–1 defeat of England in 1977 – into friendly yet heavy-drinking ambassadors for their nation at successive world cups and European championships from the late 1980s. As many have pointed out, the change in the Tartan Army had little to do with the government's anti-alcohol measures of the 1980s. Although the reasons for this change are inevitably complex, it does appear to be related to a growing sense of Scottish national identity and movement towards separation from England in political, economic and social terms. Richard Giulianotti has argued that the change in Scottish fans' behaviour is due to a 'desire to distance themselves from their English rivals and to present an image of themselves throughout Europe as the "friendly" supporters', although Irvine Welsh has also highlighted the decline in the national side's fortunes and a 'replacement of traditional working-class supporters by the nouveau riche'.[49] The way in which changing notions of Scottish national identity have led to a decline in hooliganism conversely suggests that, far from alcohol having any substantive role, English football hooliganism is closely tied to the decline of England and its Empire from the mid-1950s and the subsequent increase in overt national chauvinism and other forms of racism.

Indeed, when one looks at other sports, the alleged causal link between heavy drinking and violence is untenable. Although it is possible to object to comparisons with rugby union supporters on the basis that by and large soccer and rugby union supporters are drawn from different social classes, there is no indication that drinking before rugby league matches is any less than soccer, yet crowd violence is virtually unknown. And nowhere is alcohol consumption more conspicuous than at major darts tournaments, where crowds traditionally drink prodigious amounts of beer – it was reported that the crowd at the 1984 World Darts Championship at Jollies Club in Stoke-on-Trent drank over 55,000 pints in the eight days of the contest – yet fights or any other forms of riotous behaviour among darts spectators are non-existent. In her work on the anthropology of the horse-racing crowd, Kate Fox argues that drink plays a positive role in enhancing the sociability of the crowd: 'The behaviour of racegoers clearly indicates a relaxation of the rules which normally prevent the British from engaging in positive social interaction with strangers, and the consumption of alcohol is clearly an essential element in this process.'[50]

The draconian measures taken against alcohol had unforeseen detrimental effects on football. Sadly, it took the 1989 Hillsborough disaster to highlight that selling alcohol inside grounds could persuade spectators to come into grounds earlier, thus reducing congestion problems at turnstiles, and help improve the facilities available to football fans. The *Sun* newspaper's slander of the dead Liverpool fans as drunks who were themselves to blame for the tragedy only underlined the extent to which alcohol had become demonised. Wittingly or otherwise, the arguments of those who sought to divorce alcohol from the watching of sport in the 1970s and 1980s carried strong echoes of the ideas of the temperance campaigners of the pre-1914 period. The belief that drinking inevitably led to mayhem and violence strongly paralleled the temperance belief that alcohol automatically led to moral dissolution and a descent into despair. And underlying both views lay a fear of the 'mob' – temperance campaigners felt that the working classes' drinking habits had to be held in check in order to protect lower orders from themselves; those who sought to restrict drinking habits in the 1970s and 1980s, especially during the years of the Thatcher government, were targeting sections of the working classes whom they had identified as 'the enemy within'. Despite the fact that football hooligans and the Thatcherites shared a similar nationalistic and xenophobic world-view, the government of the time lumped together football hooligans and football supporters of all stripes with striking miners, Irish republicans and other sections of society who sought to resist it. In this they differed from the temperance movement; whereas for the early campaigners opposition to alcohol was a moral imperative which cut across all sections of society, the anti-alcohol campaigns of the late twentieth century were more selective in their targets. The huge growth of corporate hospitality during this period and the lack of any attempts to control drinking at sports identified with the middle classes demonstrated both the dual standards in operation and the falsity of the argument that drink led to violence.

Nevertheless, despite the weight of legislative and police force, the traditions of drinking at sporting events, of whatever sort, were not extinguished – on the contrary, the intense use of sporting themes in the marketing of alcohol and the associated growth of sports sponsorship would suggest that the link is as strong as ever. Indeed, the increasing importance of the television audience to modern sport and the steps taken by brewers and distillers to capture the 'couch potato' sports fan market demonstrates that the relationship of alcohol and the sports spectator, albeit one of the armchair variety, is undergoing further development. But given the long and mutually-beneficial history of the sporting crowd's love of alcohol this should come as no surprise.

Notes

1. For a contemporary look at the drinking customs of the hunt, see R. W. F. Poole, 'Field Fortifications', *Daily Telegraph*, 31 December 1999.

2. *Licensing World*, 25 July 1908; Mike Huggins, *Flat Racing and British Society 1790–1914*, London, 1999, pp. 217–18; Correspondence with Rob Street, manager of Uttoxeter Racecourse, letter dated 21 October 1999, and E.W. Gillespie, managing director of Cheltenham Racecourse, letter dated 1 September 1999.

3. *Temperance Herald*, January 1909. Guy Thorne made a similar point in 1906 in an article entitled 'Sport and Drink' in *C.B. Fry's Magazine*, vol. 5, no. 27, June 1906, pp. 196–8.

4. *Licensing World*, 30 June 1900.

5. 5 September 1900.

6. Quoted in Nicholas Fishwick, *English Football and Society 1910–1950*, Manchester, 1989, p. 60.

7. See Paul Jennings, *The Public House in Bradford 1770–1970*, Keele, 1995, p. 227.

8. Truman's Board of Directors meetings minutes, 13 October 1932 and 20 September 1956. Simonds Board Minutes, 28 November 1932.

9. Arthur Hopcraft *The Football Man*, London, 1971, Second Edition, p. 167.

10. Department of the Environment, *Football Spectator Violence. Report of an Official Working Group*, London HMSO, 1984, p. 26.

11. Mass-Observation Archive, 455 Drinking Habits, Box 7, Pub Observations 1947–48, Report: *The Influence of Football* by J.G., 7 April 1948.

12. On the same theme, see Andrew Davies, 'Leisure in the "Classic Slum" 1900–1939' in Andrew Davies and Steven Fielding (eds), *Workers' Worlds: Cultures and Communities in Manchester and Salford 1880–1939*, Manchester, 1992, pp. 105–8.

13. Terry Gourvish, *Norfolk Beers from English Barley. A History of Steward & Paterson 1793–1963*, Norwich, 1987, p. 111.

14. John Pudney, *A Draught of Contentment. The Story of the Courage Group*, London, 1971, p. 134.

15. Quoted in Gary Armstrong and Malcolm Young, 'Fanatical Football Chants: Creating and Controlling the Carnival' in *Culture, Sport, Society*, vol. 2, no. 3, Autumn 1999, p. 210. The Port Vale and Liverpool examples are from Adrian Thrills, *You're Not Singing Anymore*, London, 1998, pp. 96 and 108.

16. British Market Research Bureau Ltd, *Licensed Premises. Report on an Attitude Survey*, August 1960, prepared for the Brewers' Society, unpaginated, Tables 4a and 4b; *The Licensed Victualler*, 5 September 1900; Royal Commission On Licensing (England And Wales) 1929–31, *Report*, London, 1932, p. 159.

17. Tyneside Golf Club, *Centenary 1879–1979*, Newcastle, 1979, p. 7.

18. G. Cousins, *Golf in Britain*, London, 1975, p. 140.

19. Quoted in Peter Bills, *Passion in Exile. 100 Years of London Irish RFC*, Edinburgh, 1998, p. 109.

20. Philip Warner, *The Harlequins*, Derby, 1991, p. 188.

21. David Parry-Jones, 'Is Rugby on the Path of Soccer?' *Rugby World*, October 1980, p. 51.

22. *The Observer*, 7 February 1955.

23.   The *Guardian*, 11 November 1996. However in 1999 complaints by local residents forced the closure of Twickenham's bars after matches – see the *Guardian*, 3 February 2000 and the *Evening Standard*, 9 February 2000.

24.   John Fynlo Crellin, *'The more things change, the more they stay the same': An analysis of how Saracens and Leicester Football Clubs have managed the transition from amateur sporting clubs to professional sports businesses*, unpublished MA thesis, De Montfort University, 1999, p. 69. For Newcastle, see the *Daily Telegraph*, 26 April 1999.

25.   See, for example, Andrew Barr, *Drink. A Social History*, London, 1998, pp. 319–20.

26.   See *A Monthly Bulletin*, vol. 5, no. 1, January 1935 for a letter from 'Umpire' praising the unlimited beer available at the annual dinner of his local cricket club and arguing that this does away with snobbery. The *Bulletin* was covertly financed by the Brewers' Society.

27.   Dominic Malcolm, 'Cricket Spectator Disorder: Myths and Historical Evidence' in *The Sports Historian,* Number 19 (1) May 1999, pp. 16–37.

28.   See Keith Sandiford, *Cricket and the Victorians,* Aldershot, 1994, p. 124, and Wray Vamplew, 'Sports Crowd Disorder in Britain 1870–1914: Causes and Controls', *Journal of Sport History* (1980), no. 7.

29.   For cricket from the 1960s, see Derek Birley *A Social History of Cricket*, London, 1999, pp. 312–42. For beer sales at cricket Test matches, see *Rugby Leaguer*, 26 August 2000. For the response to the Edgbaston crowd disturbances, see the *Daily Telegraph*, 12 June, 1 July and 5 August 1998, together with letter from Mark Glithero critical of the alcohol bans on 3 August 1998.

30.   Simon Inglis, *The Football Grounds of Great Britain*, London, 1987, 2nd Edition, p. 235. Home Office Committee of Inquiry into Crowd Safety and Control at Sports Grounds, *Final Report* Cmnd. 9710, London HMSO, 1986, p. 40.

31.   Royal Commission on the Liquor Licensing Laws, *Final Report*, 1899, p. 2. For a discussion on the link between football and the decline in drunkenness, see Tony Mason, *Association Football and English Society 1863–1915*, Brighton, 1980, pp. 178–9 and Stephen Tischler, *Footballers and Businessmen*, New York, 1981, p. 134.

32.   Quoted in G.B. Wilson, *Alcohol and the Nation*, London, 1940, p. 241.

33.   Mass-Observation, *The Pub and the People*, London, 1943, pp. 304–8;*Daily Record*, April 1939, passim.

34.   Reprinted in John Moynihan, *The Soccer Syndrome*, London, 1966, p. 164.

35.   Fishwick, *English Football*, p. 62; Mass-Observation, *The Pub and the People*, p. 303.

36.   *Scottish Athletic Journal*, 21 December 1883.

37.   Royal Commission on Liquor Licensing Laws, *Final Report*, 1899, p. 24.

38.   N.L. Tranter, 'The Cappielow Riot and the Composition and Behaviour of Soccer Crowds in Late Victorian Scotland', *International Journal of the History of Sport*, vol. 12, no. 3, December 1995, pp. 132–3.

39. 19 April 1909. For background to the riot, see also Simon Craig, 'Fever Pitch, 1909' in *History Today*, May 1999, pp. 34–5.

40. Bill Murray, *The Old Firm. Sectarianism, Sport and Society in Scotland*, Edinburgh, 1984, p. 180.

41. Callum Brown, 'Sport and the Scottish Office in the Twentieth Century: The Control of a Social Problem' in J.A. Mangan (ed.), *Sport in Europe: Politics, Class, Gender*, London, 1999, pp. 178–9.

42. *Football Crowd Behaviour: Report by a Working Group Appointed by the Secretary of State for Scotland*, London HMSO, 1977. For a commentary on the Strathclyde Police findings, see Peter Marsh and Kate Fox Kilby, *Drinking and Public Disorder*, London, 1992, pp. 13–14. The findings of the West Yorkshire Police are quoted in *Public Disorder and Sporting Events: Report of a Joint Sports Council/ Social Science Research Council Panel*, London, 1978, p. 5.

43. Department of the Environment, *Football Spectator Violence. Report of an Official Working Group*, London HMSO, 1984, p. 26.

44. Home Office Committee of Inquiry into Crowd Safety and Control at Sports Grounds, *Final Report*, London HMSO, 1986, p. 40.

45. Home Office *The Hillsborough Stadium Disaster, Inquiry by the Right Hon Lord Justice Taylor, Final Report*, London HMSO, 1990, p. 9 and p. 44.

46. For beer consumption figures, John Burnett, *Liquid Pleasures. A Social History of Drinks in Modern Britain*, London, 1999, pp. 126–37.

47. E. Dunning, P. Murphy, J. Williams, *The Roots of Football Hooliganism*, London, 1988, p. 13.

48. For a broad discussion of these issues see chapter 7 of Giovanni Carnibella, Anne Fox, Kate Fox, Joe McCann, James Marsh, Peter Marsh, *Football Violence in Europe. A Report to the Amsterdam Group*, Oxford, 1996.

49. Richard Giulianotti quoted in above, p. 110; Irvine Welsh in the *Guardian*, 12 November 1999.

50. *Daily Express* 9 January 1984; *Total Sport* March 1999, pp. 45–9; Kate Fox, 'Factors influencing good crowd behaviour: A case study of British Horseracing' in *Australian Society for Sports History Bulletin*, no. 32, August 2000, p. 24.

4

A Little of What Does You Good? Alcohol, the Athlete and Sporting Performance

Writing as 'An Operator', Jonathan Badcock in 1828 published *The Fancy; or a True Sportsman's Guide*, in which he extolled the virtues of 'Captain' Barclay's training techniques for pedestrians and pugilists. In 1809 Barclay had gained fame for winning a £16,000 challenge to run a thousand miles in a thousand hours. Such a display of stamina led to his training regimen being widely adopted.[1] It included much sweating and exercise but was also concerned with diet, both food and drink. On alcohol it was stressed that the athlete's 'drink is strong ale'. Indeed,

> with respect to liquors, they must always be taken cold; and home-brewed beer, old, but not bottled, is the best. A little red wine, however, may be given to those who are not fond of malt liquor, but never more than half a pint after dinner. The quantity of beer, therefore, should not exceed three pints during the whole day, and it must be taken with breakfast and dinner, no supper being allowed. Water is never given alone, and ardent spirits are strictly prohibited, however diluted.

Cider was also recommended as the base for a sweating liquor.[2] In part contrast to Badcock's advice, a modern, detailed study of *Bell's Life in London* argues that in the late eighteenth up to at least the mid-nineteenth century spirits especially were regarded as strength-giving.[3] The debate, however, was on whether spirits were good or bad for the athlete, not if alcohol itself should be proscribed.

Alcohol was also used during sporting performances. The bottle holders at prize fights were instructed by the editor of *Bell's Life in London*, Vincent Dowling, that

> a small quantity of water is sufficient to wash his mouth, and this ought not to be swallowed ... A bottle of brandy-and-water should be in readiness when a stimulant becomes necessary after long exertion, but this should be used with moderation; and at times, especially

in wet, cold weather, about a table-spoon of neat brandy may be given – this ought to be of the best quality.[4]

No doubt at times alcohol was consumed to provide the fighters with extra 'bottom' or courage. Not all alcohol in the ring was drunk. In 1825 during a fight near Warwick between Jem Ward and Tom Cannon a crowd of 15,000 saw 'Spring (the bottle holder) lift the helpless man on to Cribb's (the second) knee, and blow brandy up Tom's nostrils; but it was no go'.[5] There are many references to alcohol being consumed during long-distance running and walking performances. For example Lieutenant Fairman of the Royal Lancashire Militia went 60 miles in 13 hours 33 minutes in 1804 and en route took a piece of bread steeped in madeira.[6] Foster Powell, famous for his walks from London to York and back in less than six days, was reported usually to take wine and water or brandy and water during his perambulations.[7] As in pugilism, not all alcohol was drunk. During his 60-mile walk Lieutenant Fairman took a break after 49 miles in which he was 'rubbed down with hot towels, his feet soaked in warm water, and his body bathed all over with spirits'.[8]

The use of alcohol by athletes should be seen in the context of a society in which many of the population utilised alcoholic drinks as thirst quenchers or for physical stamina. Such drinks were seen as less dangerous than water which was both scarce and unsafe in rural areas and even more contaminated in the urban. Alcoholic drinks at least relied on water either drawn from unpolluted deep wells or which had been boiled as part of the brewing process. Moreover it was generally believed that intoxicants imparted stamina: whenever extra energy was needed resort was had to alcohol. Agricultural employers provided drink to fuel exertion at harvest time and indeed Francis Place, the political activist, claimed in 1834 that almost all men in strenuous occupations obtained their energy from intoxicants.[9]

Such ideas took a long time to change. At the turn of the century some endurance athletes were still using alcohol as an aid. In the United States in October 1900 Margaret Gast cycled 2,600 miles in only thirteen days during which she supplemented her diet with small quantities of alcohol in the form of ale and brandy.[10] The 1904 Olympic marathon winner, Thomas Hicks, survived the gruelling St Louis event by imbibing brandy laced with strychnine.[11] In Europe too long-distance runners and 24-hour cyclists made use of alcohol for refreshment and to reduce the sense of fatigue. The former consumed cognac and the latter rum and champagne.[12] In his *Principles of Training for Amateur Athletics* of 1892 H. L. Curtis suggested moderate consumption of alcohol as part of a sportsman's regime but warned against smoking and coffee. Although their game was less strenuous than either running or cycling, cricketers too resorted to alcohol during a day's play. At the end of the nineteenth century they were being advised that when playing on a hot day 'beer and stout are too heady and heavy' and 'gin and ginger beer is too sickly sweet' and that 'shandy-gaff, sherry or claret, and soda are the most thirst-quenching, the lightest and the cleanest to the palate'.[13] Had the Yorkshire bowler, Bobby Peel only heeded this advice he might not have been dismissed from the county side for being so much under the influence that in 1896 he allegedly watered the wicket in unorthodox fashion![14]

But the times they were a changing, albeit slowly. By 1888 in his advice to athletes Montague Shearman leaned towards the increasing trans-Atlantic tendency to adopt 'the system of training upon water alone, and taking no alcohol in any shape during training'. He left it to doctors to decide if alcohol was 'nutritious to any degree' but noted that it was universally acknowledged 'that it is very hard to digest, and this alone should be a strong argument against its use'. Nevertheless he accepted that if a sportsman was 'accustomed to drink beer or wine, it is a hard thing to say that the athlete should give up either and take to water if he doesn't like it'. He had seen men well trained 'upon beer, upon claret, and upon weak whisky-and-water'. However, he warned that 'any other wines . . . are bad in training, as they excite the nerves and interfere with sound and quiet sleep'. He allowed that 'if a man is getting stale, good strengthening wine may do him a world of good', though he stressed that 'as long as an athlete is not in this state, the glass or two of port', which he often recommended to take, 'is exceedingly likely to do harm, and can hardly do any good'. All in all the 'general principle' should be 'the less alcohol . . . the better'.[15]

On the other hand the Reverend Beveridge, writing in the *Scottish Athletic Journal* in 1882, was adamant that 'much liquid of any kind ought not to be imbibed by the training athlete; and there is one kind of liquid which must not be imbibed at all, namely that which is alcoholic in its nature. There is no use whatever of a man going into training if he intends, at the same time to use intoxicating liquors.'[16] The teetotal lobby claimed that 'medical science has proved beyond a doubt the injuriousness of spirituous liquors to the human frame'.[17] Clearly the advice being provided for sportspersons was confusing and contradictory. An article in the *Scottish Football Annual* for 1889/90 suggested that

there can be no harm in a glass or two of sound ale or a little light wine such as hock or claret at dinner. The glass of port afterwards I confess I think unnecessary as long as the training process is well borne. If, however, a man shows any sign of falling with the state known as 'overtrained', that is to say, when the reducing process is too rapid or too severe, a little port or dry champagne at meals may be found beneficial. Spirits should be strictly abstained from, as they tend to prevent the elimination of carbonic acid.[18]

The rowing expert, R.C. Lehman, noted that the Oxford boat-race crew in the 1890s were allowed a glass of draught beer or claret and water with their lunch, two glasses with their dinner, and a glass of port with their dessert. Occasionally, champagne could be substituted for the other drinks, but only when they had 'been doing very hard work, or when they show evident signs of being over-fatigued, and require a fillip'.[19] Even in the 1920s English cricketer Fred Root, after an arduous stint of bowling in the Fourth Test against Australia, was advised by the Chairman of Selectors, P.F. Warner, to utilise the brine baths at Droitwich and drink an occasional bottle of champagne.[20]

As has been shown in the chapter on brewery involvement in sport, the 1880s saw the start of adverts professing the fitness-aiding qualities of alcohol. Grant's Morella Cherry Brandy claimed that it 'strengthened and invigorated the system', as was proved by its use by Captain Boyton whilst swimming the Straits of Dover.[21] Indeed the gallant captain was quoted as finding it 'not only palatable and refreshing, but most effective in keeping up nerve and strength'. Prior to the First World War the *Licensed Trade News,* published in Birmingham, was countering the abstinence push by arguing that 'the whole field of physical culture is filled with the best of men doing the best of work on alcohol in moderation'. It recommended 'a good sound, wholesome glass of beer, there is nothing to come near it as a thirst quencher, a dietetic, a support and a stimulant'.[22] As we have seen, the medicinal qualities of alcohol were still being proclaimed in advertising campaigns in the interwar years, most notably in the Brewers' Society slogan 'Beer is Best' and Guinness's explicit promotion of itself as being good for strength from 1929 to 1949.[23] Nevertheless by this time athletes were generally being advised not to consume intoxicants on any scale as they were considered detrimental to sporting performance. Viscount Knebworth's advice to aspiring boxers in the early 1930s was that 'any large consumption of alcohol is out of the question, but alcohol in moderation is a fine aid to the digestion. A glass of wine or a glass of beer with his supper does nobody any harm . . . But no-one in training for a boxing match can afford to drink anything but a very minimum of alcoholic liquid.'[24] He was supported by Dr Alphonse Abrahams who maintained that 'alcohol may be given as a medicine, but a healthy athlete should not require medicine therefore alcohol is not needed for him'. Interestingly, and a portent of a modern argument for sportspersons to drink, he also declared ' the practice of giving champagne to the University boat crews serves some useful purpose in lessening the anxiety which often prevails before a race'.[25] By the mid-1960s the Senior Registrar at the Medical Rehabilitation Centre in London was counselling that 'alcohol taken immediately prior to competition is inadvisable'.[26] In the 1970s there were some claims that alcoholic products, beers especially, were good sources of carbohydrates and were also useful in replenishing body fluid lost during training and competition, but nutritionists have shown that neither was done effectively or efficiently.[27]

Today it is recognised that alcohol depresses the nervous system, impairs both motor ability and judgement, reduces endurance, and, as a diuretic, can disturb electrolyte balance and cause dehydration, all of which are detrimental to effective sports performance.[28] In 1982 the American College of Sports Medicine conducted an analysis of the effects of alcohol on physical performance and argued that it had four main adverse effects.[29] First, the acute ingestion of alcohol deleteriously influences many psychomotor skills in a dose-related manner, thus negatively affecting reaction time, eye-hand co-ordination, accuracy and balance: in tracking tasks, such as driving, control movements lose their smoothness and precision. Second, alcohol consumption significantly influences physiological functions crucial to physical performance such as respiratory dynamics and cardiac activity. Third, the ingestion of alcohol does not improve muscular work capacity and indeed may decrease performance levels. Finally, because alcohol dilates the blood vessels close to the surface of the skin, it can impair temperature regulation during prolonged exercise in a cold environment: drinking from a hip flask on the ski slopes may produce an inner glow but it enhances the risk of hypothermia. Additionally alcohol has an anti-coagulant effect which could aggravate blood loss in some injuries.[30] Many athletes, of course, would not require this detailed scientific work to demonstrate what was patently obvious from personal experience or observation. There is some debate as to whether moderate alcohol consumption can improve isometric muscular strength. Experiments in the early 1960s suggested that it could have an effect similar to the response achieved by loud vocal encouragement, but there is now considerable scepticism at this finding which has proved difficult to replicate.[31]

Nonetheless there are those who believe that there are sporting benefits to alcohol consumption that outweigh the negative aspects. Although generally alcohol has adverse effects on performance in sports that require fast reactions, complex decision-making, and highly-skilled actions, it is considered to have a positive influence on performance where there is an advantage to be gained from its use as an anti-tremor aid, as an isometric muscular strengthener, and as an anti-anxiety drug. For some individuals it is simply that small amounts of alcohol can reduce feelings of insecurity and tension and improve self-confidence. For some teams too the psychological and other aspects of drinking together may have positive outcomes. Tactical discussions in the bar at the end of a day's play – common among cricketers – is one example.[32] The great Spurs football side of the 1960s used to meet in the back room of the Bell and Hare, just off the ground, to dissect every move of the last game and look ahead to the next.[33] Team bonding by drinking together is another obvious example. Pat Nevin, ex-chairman of the Professional Footballers Association, maintains that at the start of the football season such bonding is more desired by managers than absolute fitness.[34] Teams are collections of individuals who may not necessarily get along with each other. On top of personality differences, there is the friction brought about by competition for places. Older players may be wary of newcomers, unwilling to pass on the lessons of experience for fear that it might hasten their journey down the inclined plane to sporting oblivion. The young bloods, aware that few of them will become established in the team, may not assist each other as much the coach might desire. The team itself is regularly changing its composition. Alcohol is sometimes regarded as a panacea to this problem, in that drinking together is seen as a way of bonding team-mates. Such sessions are often instigated by the older 'pros' but approved of by the club. Tony Parkes, who played for Spurs, Gillingham, Brentford, Queens Park Rangers, Fulham, West Ham, Stoke, Falkirk, Blackpool and Halifax Town, found that drinking sessions were used at all these clubs as a forum to air grievances and give accolades.[35] In the 1980s Liverpool Football Club, one of the dominant teams of the decade, used to hold social drinking sessions one Monday each month policed by the senior players.[36] Ron Atkinson, one of Britain's more successful managers in the last three decades, accepted that 'drinking among team-mates . . . creates dressing-room spirit'.[37] Indeed, even when he was a non-League manager at Kettering in the early 1970s, he insisted on buying the team a round of drinks on the way back from successful away games. He also persuaded the directors of the importance of an end-of-season trip to Majorca for the whole team to wind down together with 'laughs, not much sleep, and a severe case of mass bacardi poisoning'!38 Generally, however, he stressed that drinking should be in moderation. It was not just in football that clubs initiated drinking sessions for their players. When the Australian test cricketer, David Boon, took charge at Durham, he encouraged the players to go out to the pub together to chat and have a meal.[39]

For most participants sport is a recreational stress reliever, but for elite athletes it can be a stress-creator, often producing severe pre-competition anxiety. Not all athletes can cope unaided with this and some have resorted to anti-anxiety drugs, including alcohol. That sherry was a useful pre-match drink was a prevalent belief in rugby in the 1950s and 1960s: at noon on match days Jeff Butterfield, an England rugby union back, drank a pint pot of raw eggs and sherry[40] and as late as 1989 Australian rugby league player Andrew Ettingshausen noted that a sherry bottle was passed around the Leeds rugby league dressing room before matches.[41] The communal whisky bottle too has featured in football changing rooms prior to the game.[42] Leighton Rees, the Welsh international darts player, reckoned that a couple of pints of beer helped steel him up for a match.[43] Another Welsh darts thrower, Alan Evans, credited his success in the 1974 Watneys British Open to drinking seven pints of lager (not a Watneys product!) before the final.[44] Dr Tom Crisp, a medical officer for the British team at the Atlanta Olympic Games, believes 'that there may even be benefits [to drinking a week or so] before a major competition in terms of relaxation and social interaction . . . I think if you look at professional sportsmen they are under a great deal of pressure, and alcohol is quite a good way of relaxing.'[45]

Some sports require steady hands as well as steady nerves. The sedative effect of alcohol can be useful where a firm stance and a reduced heart rate could be important. Predominantly these are 'aiming' sports such as shooting, archery, snooker, darts and fencing. However, there is greater benefit where the apparatus involved puts least pressure on the arm, so darts throwers gain more than pistol shooters who are better off than archers.[46] Reaction times are, however, slowed by alcohol consumption so there is no tradition of its use in aiming sports with moving targets such as clay-pigeon shooting.[47] Although bar-room sports have a reputation for heavy drinking by its participants, the technique that has developed among the more successful is one of regular small 'topping up' doses of alcohol so as to avoid fluctuating blood alcohol concentrations.[48]

In horse racing alcohol is seen as offering two specific kinds of help to jockeys. Many of them drink champagne before going into the sauna in the belief that it helps them sweat.[49] Traditionally too the French sparkling wine has been used to keep down their weight. In the first half of the nineteenth century Frank Butler, the first Triple Crown winner, followed a diet of champagne to help restrict his weight to 8 stone 7 pounds.[50] Later in that century, Fred Archer, champion jockey for thirteen successive seasons, allegedly breakfasted on a diet of castor oil, a biscuit and a small glass of champagne for the bulk of his racing life.[51] In more modern times Lester Piggott, champion on eleven occasions, also used champagne in this way but with the occasional gin and tonic as a change.[52] Although nutrition research indicates that, as alcohol contains calories, drinking can impair any weight reduction programme even if food intake is reduced, the very small amounts that jockeys take can be seen simply as a tasty and perhaps psychologically satisfying alternative to food.[53]

Alcohol has become a prohibited substance in some sports but not all. Those that are part of the Olympic programme have to abide by International

Olympic Committee regulations that list alcohol as one of the classes of drugs subject to certain restrictions. There is no total ban across all sports as alcohol is normally regarded as inimical to performance, but it is proscribed in shooting, archery, fencing and the relevant parts of the modern pentathlon. Those sports that are not recognised by the IOC are left to their own devices; thus in both snooker and darts the relevant association makes the decision, which currently is to allow the consumption of alcohol, though behind the scenes rather than in public view.

The UK Sports Council has legislated against the use of alcohol as a performance-enhancing drug in those areas where there is an advantage to be gained. This caused some consternation in archery circles where there was a fear that recreational archers might leave the sport. The National Council accepted that as alcohol was on the banned substances list they should notify all archers via the rulebook and then it was up to the archers themselves to decide whether or not to partake of alcohol at tournaments. If they did so then they would have to accept the possible consequences. Nevertheless it was also decided that judges should have their authority strengthened by the addition of a rule which would allow them to stop an archer shooting if he or she is considered to be jeopardising safety.[54]

Other bodies, notably the Jockey Club, have been less concerned with performance enhancement than with the deleterious effects of drink on sportspersons including the danger that alcohol-affected activity can have on other participants. There are instances where jockeys have ridden under the influence. Ron Barry did so at Uttoxeter in 1973, the day after he had failed to recover from the previous night's celebration of his Cheltenham Gold Cup victory. Surprisingly he still won, by two and a half lengths on 9–1 shot Pneuma.[55] Yet, although the idea of a drunk or drugged jockey aboard a horse is a frightening one, the Jockey Club took no action on this issue till October 1994 when, at the instigation of Michael Turner, their new chief medical adviser, a protocol was developed for the testing of riders for banned substances. These included marijuana, cocaine, amphetamines and alcohol, the threshold for the latter being set at the drink-driving limit.[56]

Sporting Culture and Alcohol Abuse

These days alcohol is certainly not recommended by sports scientists, but its use by sportspersons does not cause much concern relative to other performance-enhancing drugs. Most concerns that there is focus on the danger that drinking alcohol could cause sportspersons to lose too much control. It is behaviour off the field that really attracts opprobrium. Here alcohol is probably the substance most abused by sportspersons. Although there is a conflict between sporting excellence and alcohol consumption, paradoxically teetotallers are in the minority in modern British sport.[57] The question to be answered is why should so many sportspersons opt to drink as well as play? Clearly in the long run excessive drinking is inimical to sports performance. A liver damaged by hepatitis or destroyed by cirrhosis is not conducive to effective sports participation, or indeed in the worst cases participation in sport at all. However, most sportspersons – even those who drink to excess – never have to confront this situation as they retire from active sports participation before their drinking has such consequences. It is the short-run, deleterious effects that are openly risked.

With their physical prowess and fitness, young athletes in particular may see themselves as immune from the addictive and adverse effects of alcohol. Certainly sportsmen can disguise the level of their alcohol consumption because of their physical fitness.[58] In the mid-nineteenth century 'Stonehenge', a writer on rural sports, cited instances of young men drinking one to two gallons of strong ale a day for many months 'without any great injury'. It was, he added, 'astonishing what quantities of intoxicating drinks may be imbibed without much injury, provided that a corresponding amount of exercise is taken'.[59] Australian rugby league player, Ken Thornett, recalled that on occasions when playing in England in the early 1950s he had 'drunk seven or eight pints of Tetley's bitter on a Friday night and played well enough the next day'.[60] Jimmy Greaves, then an alcoholic English football international, noted that 'people would see me competing at sport and never believe that they were watching somebody who within the past forty-eight hours had knocked back two bottles of vodka and a couple of gallons of beer'. [61] Paul Merson of Arsenal and England was able to win the Young Player of the Year award in 1989 despite long late-night drinking sessions and the dazzling Irish and Manchester United winger George Best always claimed that he could party all night then strut his stuff on the pitch.[62] It may be of course that in some sports, especially team ones, the adverse effects of drinking are not so obvious as in say marathon running or other endurance sports.

Some sportspersons perhaps are not persuaded that the case against moderate drinking has been established. Certainly it is less publicised than that against excessive imbibing and indeed the evidence suggests that such consumption has neither beneficial nor detrimental effects on physical performance and that light drinking even on the night before competition will not significantly diminish performance the following morning.[63] One publication, endorsed by the Director of the National Coaching Foundation, notes that 'there is little evidence to suggest that a moderate consumption of alcohol in a social environment will impair performance'.[64] The difficulty in all this is to distinguish where moderate consumption merges into excessive consumption, which, most likely, is detrimental to performance. We have no idea how many sportspeople find that moderate levels of drinking eventually lead to addiction and more serious levels of consumption.

It should be stressed that British sportspeople exist within a society in which, subject to age limits, alcohol is a socially accepted drug. Not to drink is to exhibit deviant behaviour! Alcohol consumption becomes engrained in leisure activities. In such an environment drinking becomes established as a sporting tradition be it the stirrup cup prior to the hunt setting off, the buying of a round to celebrate a hole-in-one at golf, or the champagne sprayed over the winner of a motor race. Like other members of society sportspersons use alcohol for relaxation, to relieve stress, and for convivial recreational purposes: certainly the 'nineteenth' is the most popular hole at most golf clubs. Historically some sports organisations such as the Royal Caledonian Hunt Club were in effect drinking clubs more concerned with the quality of the wine than that of the horses.[65] Amateur sports teams have a long tradition of treating each other to refreshments, alcoholic or otherwise, after a match. That so many early football and cricket clubs were attached to public houses by sponsorship, changing rooms, or ground provision both encouraged and facilitated this,[66] although it was not always equitably arranged. Forfar Athletic in 1890 arranged to have its own players supplied with 'half a bottle of whisky and one bottle of port', but restricted the visitors to 'a pie and a pint of ale apiece'.[67] Possibly, of course, this treating was a means of paying supposedly amateur players. Significantly the move into professionalism in football in the late nineteenth century undermined the alcoholic reciprocity between clubs, though Dumbarton, for one, elected to continue the after-match socials whenever the opposing team was agreeable, as they felt 'that it would be a pity should it ever be considered necessary – on account of the demands of professionalism, or for any other reason – to eliminate every source of relaxation and enjoyment from the life of the football player, and reduce the game to a mere sordid pursuit'.[68] County cricketer, Fred Root noted that there were plenty of 'thirst-quenching opportunities' in police cricket matches in the 1920s, a fact that would be appreciated by Root and other imbibing fast bowlers.[69] As we have seen in previous chapters, the bar has become a major source of revenue for many sports clubs. From the outset of Leamington Rugby Club in 1926 there was a bar. Initially simply a table from which bottles of beer were sold, by the late 1990s it generated gross profits of £66,000, some six times the amounts raised from members' subscriptions.[70] At the Goring and Streatley Golf Club bar takings produced 6 per cent of the club's revenue in 1938, a proportion that had risen to 11 per cent by 1994.[71] Effect has become cause as the importance of the bar has given sports clubs the incentive to encourage members and players to drink.

Many of the sportspersons who drink are well aware of the negative influence that alcohol can have on their sporting function, but often those involved are not concerned with achieving their best possible performance. They are participating for fun, aiming to win but not at the sacrifice of the social side of their chosen sport or club. Sunday league football with teams such as Real Ale Madrid and PSV Hangover, whose matches end before opening time and often have their changing rooms in a local pub, are a prime example here.[72] Similarly Justin Langer, the Australian test cricketer, has observed that English league cricket is a place 'to learn more about enjoying a pint of beer and having a few laughs' than to develop the skills to become a contender for the first class game.[73] Duncan Stewart has argued that drinking is almost a membership norm in many amateur sports and Tom Reilly has identified rugby, squash and water polo as sports where there is such a social convention and peer group pressure to drink alcohol both after training and matches and at club functions.[74] Certainly biographies of both elite and social players testify to the drinking culture of rugby union, a trait shared by spectators of that game as illustrated by leading sports magazines in both Britain and Australia producing guides of where to drink before and after games during the 1999 World Cup.[75] Many women who play rugby union also appear to have adopted this cultural attitude and aspire to emulate the male members of their club in drinking feats.[76] Sportswomen are also consuming alcohol outside rugby. A recent book on women's football has indirectly shown that a drinking culture has emerged among elite players in that game.[77] What cannot be distinguished is whether the participants in a sports drinking culture would have been drinking irrespective of being involved in sport; whether sport simply provided an opportunity and companions to drink with; and whether these same companions would have been chosen outside a sporting environment.

Sportspersons sometimes abuse alcohol. Populist press exposés of alcohol-fuelled misdemeanours by modern footballers provide a seemingly endless catalogue of hotel smashing, sexual impropriety and drunken driving.[78] This tabloid evidence is incontrovertible but raises two issues of interpretation. First is the question of how much of this may simply be deemed as newsworthy because the men concerned are footballers. Clearly some sportsmen – on the town, free of partner, with money in their pockets – do stupid things under the influence of alcohol, but then so do many young men: and that is what most sportsmen are. Yet the alcohol-fuelled antics of the majority of miscreants go unreported so we do not know whether or not the relationship of footballers with alcohol is in any way unique. Secondly the intrusion of the media into the private lives of players is relatively new so temporal comparisons cannot be made. However, there is some suggestion that misbehaviour by inebriated footballers is nothing new. In 1883 the *Scottish Athletic Journal* criticised the 'high jinks in hotels by football teams [that] are becoming such a nuisance that something must be done to put an end to the gross misconduct which goes on'.[79] Five years earlier two Queens Park players had been fined 20 shillings each for disorderly conduct after a victorious match in Nottingham.[80] Indeed trips down south of the border, usually taken at New Year or Easter, allegedly often resulted in 'drunken orgies'.[81] At the end of the century it was claimed that 'nearly every club in Glasgow had had from time to time difficulties with its players because of the intemperance by which they are beset'.[82] Then there is the Heart of Midlothian goalkeeper who let in seven goals when in 'a peculiar condition'.[83] South of the border things were no better. Writing somewhat ungrammatically in 1909 Jimmy Wilson of Preston North End noted that 'we all know the bugbear of a footballer's career is alcohol . . . perhaps it is not generally known to how great an extent such a state of affairs does exist. One has only to make his way to one or two well-known hotels to see it for themselves.'[84] H.G. Norris of Fulham maintained that players 'are not always fit to undergo ninety minutes of strenuous football on Saturdays, due to indiscretions committed during the previous week, the greatest and most frequent cause being drink'. In his opinion 'intoxicating drink has been the downfall of only too many football players'.[85]

It was not just in football that overindulgence appears to have occurred. One perspective on Victorian professional golfers can be gleaned from a letter in *The Field* in October 1881. The writer, signing himself 'Scratch Medal' wrote:

> Will you allow me to draw attention to one serious evil which has almost invariably accompanied the most scientific golf – that is, professional golf? I refer to the almost universal drunkenness with which it is attended. The evil has two sides to it – one, the moral side, as to which I will only say this, that I never could quite understand how those who appreciate the healthy charm of this noble game could find it in their hearts, I will not say to encourage, but not to do their best to discourage, the vice, which has been to many a brilliant professional golfer now alive the cause of almost complete ruin. The other is the scientific side. I hardly suppose that anyone would argue that a man who is drunk in the evening can play steady golf the next day.

He went on to make the suggestions that 'treating' should be much more sparingly indulged in than it is and that clubs offering prizes to professionals should take some steps 'to prevent the money given in prizes finding its way direct to the pockets of the resident publicans'. The difficulty with this 'evidence' is that it comes from a particular standpoint and may simply reflect a middle-class moral panic. Even if true, does it reflect class behaviour or a sporting one?

By the early twentieth century, when tournament and exhibition matches were becoming more regular, the leading professional golfers were more abstemious. Scotsman James Braid, five times winner of the Open Championship, was a believer in regular work habits, regular exercise and a lot of sleep; he did not smoke and drank very little. In preparation for the 1911 Open, his fifth of six titles, Jerseyman Harry Vardon allowed himself only one whisky and four pipes of tobacco a day.[86] That said, a reading of many golf club histories, however, does suggest that several club professionals continued to risk their careers by drinking, perhaps because of the opportunities that arose when doubling as bar steward. Ramsay Hunter of Royal St Georges is a case in point. Employed as club professional, greenkeeper and caddie superintendent, he was demoted to greenkeeper in 1899 because of his drinking and then was sacked for repeating the offence.[87]

Nevertheless it may be that footballers have always had more opportunity than most professional sportsmen to indulge in drinking. Unlike golfers, who had to spend most of their time on course maintenance and playing with club members, and cricketers, who often had a full day's play several times a week with travel to follow, professional footballers have always had time on their hands given the training regimes operated by many clubs that demanded attendance at the ground for only a few hours a day. Indeed a typical pre-1914 training programme would involve nothing at all on Monday; on other days a 10.00 a.m. arrival time with a brisk 5-mile walk to follow unless the weather was inclement when there might be skipping or Indian club and punchball work.[88] Little changed over the century. As Mick Quinn, footballer turned racehorse trainer, noted: 'footballers have time to kill. Time to go to the bookies, pub or snooker club. They have the afternoon and whole night.'[89] The situation has been accentuated in more modern times with the abolition of wage restraint and the spiralling of earnings. Football manager, Ron Atkinson, recalls some hard drinkers in the immediate pre-Second World War period, but he is also of the view that in the past couple of generations of players there has been a change with some 'wild drinking' by young star players whom he has seen 'at certain football functions quite literally drinking themselves into oblivion'.[90] Long-serving manager, Bobby Robson, has also seen 'booze as one of the major evils of the game. And its influence has become more widespread now there is big money to be earned.'[91] Mark Bennett of the charity Alcohol Concern puts it clearly: 'when you get young men earning enormous sums of money, with enormous amounts of free time and a heavy drinking culture, you have some key indications for an alcohol problem'.[92] Yet popular sportsmen have never had to rely on buying their own drinks. Fans have always been willing to buy drinks for their heroes. In the 1890s county cricket administrators complained about the public buying drinks for their cricketing heroes, one of the downsides of players remaining close to their communities.[93] Indeed the Yorkshire chairman claimed that the 'demon drink' had cost his side the county championship and the Warwickshire secretary went so far as to appeal to the public not to treat the county's professionals.[94] Bill Appleyard of Newcastle United, in *Thomson's Weekly News* in February 1902, and John Cameron, one-time secretary of the Players' Union, writing in *Spaldings Football Annual* four years later, both felt that treating by admirers was a great temptation to footballers.[95]

Then there are those who allow alcohol to abuse them. 'In the early hours of a frosty winter's morning . . . I was ransacking the dustbin . . . for empty vodka bottles . . . and finished up kneeling by the side of the dustbin draining the last drops out of the bottles.'[96] With those words English international, Jimmy Greaves, was the first professional footballer to admit publicly that he had an alcohol problem. More recently he has been followed by England captain, Tony Adams, earlier jailed for a drink driving offence, and his then Arsenal team-mate, Paul Merson who was also addicted to cocaine.[97] Others never openly acknowledged their drinking problems, but it is generally accepted that Tommy Caton, the Manchester City, Arsenal and Charlton defender, drank himself to death on two bottles of spirits a day; that Jim Baxter, Rangers and Scotland crowd pleaser, had a liver transplant aged fifty-five after years of hard drinking; and that Albert Johanneson, the first black player to appear in a Wembley cup final, died, also aged fifty-five, of alcohol-related causes.[98] George Best, the mercurial Irish winger, has never overcome his drinking troubles and the jury is still out on Paul Gascoigne who has been hospitalised several times for treatment.

Few sports seem to have been immune from the abuse of alcohol by participants. Pugilist Henry Pearce, the 'Game Chicken', made 'too free with his constitution' and 'in company with sporting men frequently he poured down copious libations at the shrine of Bacchus' so that 'his health was impaired'.[99] Apocryphal stories abound for nineteenth-century horse racing. Jem Snowden is said to have turned up a week late for Chester races; Charles Marlow to have lost a two-horse race for the 1850 Doncaster Cup on the odds-on favourite Voltigeur through lack of sobriety; and, after a morning at the brandy bottle, Bill Scott is alleged to have been so drunk at the Derby of 1846 that he did not realise that the race had started.[100] Nevertheless it is clear that Scott, winner of nine St Legers, and George Fordham, fourteen times champion jockey, were alcoholics as was Tommy Loates, champion in three seasons towards the end of the century, Bernard Dillon, the Derby-winning rider in 1910, and perhaps American Skeets Martin who tended to 'hit the bottle'.[101] Jump jockey Bobby Beasley triumphed over his alcoholism to win the Cheltenham Gold Cup in 1974.[102] In the modern era both Walter Swinburn and Steve Cauthen have acknowledged having drinking problems.[103] Indoors, Jimmy White, generally acknowledged as the best player never to have won a world title, has had major drink problems to overcome.[104]

That such high-profile sportsmen had alcohol problems does not mean that their chosen profession can be held responsible for their predicament. Individual character flaws or personality deficiencies are not the prerogative of a sporting life. The 1994 General Household Survey showed that about one in ten male drinkers and one in twenty female drinkers had an alcohol problem in that they exhibited at least two physical or psychological symptoms of alcohol dependency. More generally 27 per cent of men and 13 per cent of women were drinking more than the recommended limits, at that time 21 units a week for men and 14 for women.[105] Alcohol is embedded in British culture. Hence it is difficult to establish whether or not professional sportspersons are different from the rest of the population, or sections of it, in their resort to alcohol and descent into problem drinking. Nearly 90 per cent of the adult population admits to drinking alcohol and one in five drink more than the recommended safe level.[106] In 1998 a survey of 1,800 British companies reported alcohol 'misuse' by staff, but unfortunately the questionnaire did not provide a definition of 'misuse'.[107] The charity Alcohol Concern claims that one person in twenty is an alcoholic but again no definition was given.[108]

It may well be the case that some people are genetically predisposed to addiction or alcoholism but according to Stephen Stephens, Director of the Addictions Unit at Marchmont Priory Hospital, Southampton, 'the fact is that we don't really know why some people become addicts and others don't'.[109] Henri Begleiter, an American researcher, estimates that genes perhaps account for only 40–60 per cent of the risk of alcoholism, though they do not ensure that it will happen.[110] Whether sportspersons have a greater tendency than other occupational groups to become alcoholics is uncertain given the currently inadequate statistical information, but there are certainly features of a career in sport that might encourage its emergence in those players predisposed towards it.[111]

In some sports there are job specific issues. There is an expectation in professional football that players will turn out even when injured and in pain.[112] In cricket there is the boredom of what could be at one time a seven-days-a-week job, though fortunately this is now less often the case.[113] The low weights required in horse racing can cause problems as the effects of alcohol are often aggravated by the lack of food. Indeed nutrition expert Professor Michael Lean suggests that 'alcoholism is a probable effect of being starved'.[114] Allegedly both Cauthen and Swinburn were bulimic and had alcohol-related problems. For other jockeys alcohol abuse is a product of a stressful life. Few would argue with the claim of ex-champion Frankie Dettori that 'being a jockey is a pressure job, and when things don't go well, you take your losers home'.[115] No one is immune. In the year that he was champion Doug Smith once went over 100 rides without a winner. Graham Thorner, National Hunt champion rider in 1971, reckoned 'the worst thing about the job was the periods of depression when I couldn't ride a winner'.[116] Moreover, every time jockeys race they are subject to public and employer appraisal; they are constantly watching their weight; and they anticipate injury each time they get on a horse. No wonder some jockeys appear to have used alcohol either to escape reality or as a painkiller. National Hunt riders, with notable exceptions such as teetotallers Tony McCoy (despite being sponsored by Guinness), Jonjo O'Neill and John Francome, see drinking as part of the social life associated with their sport, and regard it as a means of winding down.[117]

More generally there is no place to hide on the sports field. Every time they go out to play sportspersons are subject to public and professional appraisal; and often their performance depends not just on themselves but on their team-mates and on the opposition.[118] Jimmy Greaves drank heavily when with Spurs in the 1960s 'to help relieve the pressures of big-time football'.[119] Nevertheless Greaves himself still maintained that 'there is no harm whatsoever in young sportsmen drinking in moderation. A relaxing hour in a pub with your team-mates after a hard game or tough training session can be the best possible wind-down and escape valve from the immense pressure of modern football.'[120] A major problem with Merson in his early career was a lack of confidence so severe that he actually had palpitations on the pitch; alcohol helped him gain confidence on the field and overcome his shyness off it.[121] Pat Nevin, one-time chairman of the Professional Footballers' Association (PFA), argues that when off-form players are booed by the crowd, castigated in the media, and have their families harassed by fans '. . . one of the reasons why players turn to a few drinks is to cope with [this] stress'.[122] Mickey Thomas, the Welsh international, 'had no privacy' and took to drink 'to get away from' the attention.[123] Cricket is a team game within which the individual is often isolated, worrying about his own form even in the midst of team success. As is clear from David Frith's study of cricketing suicides, some could not handle the stress of perpetual uncertainty and turned to drink.[124]

Constant insecurity is the hallmark of a career in professional sport. Insecurity stems from many sources including fear of injury, loss of form, threats to jobs from newcomers, and the inevitable short shelf life of professional sportsmen. Every day the professional faces the possibility of no work tomorrow: losing in a tight finish, dropping an important catch, being injured in a tackle could all lead to non-selection. Historically too there was, and for some players still is, the annual trauma of contract renewal. In 1891 the Football League Management Committee forbad the signing of players for more than a season at a time.[125] Some cricketers managed to secure longer than annual contracts before 1914 but these were a rarity and continued to be so. Writing in the 1930s, English professional cricketer Fred Root remarked on the 'extreme anxiety' among young players brought about by counties often delaying their announcements on future engagements until the middle of winter.[126] Most jockeys, even today, do not have retainers and have to compete for mounts in a vastly oversupplied labour market.[127] Moreover in many cases the professional has no control over his own destiny. A new manager or chairperson can lead to redundancy. Seniority offers no security: there are always rivals for his position and the decision as to the relative abilities of the old hand and the newcomer is made by others. Economy campaigns too can lead to dismissal. Historically Bolton Wanderers pared their playing staff in 1898 with the aim of saving £1,200 and when Lancashire County Cricket Club embarked on a wave of retrenchment in 1912 several players were sacked 'solely on the grounds of economy'.[128] Although the restrictions have now eased, historically too it was not easy for professionals in several sports to voluntarily change their employer. To switch from one county to another necessitated a two year's residential qualification for cricketers and in football the retain and transfer system severely curbed the economic freedom of players.[129]

Then there is the question of retirement, often involuntary and generally at an early age relative to conventional retirees. For some retirement comes even earlier than expected because of the socially-sanctioned violence on the field which can cause career-ending damage. Even in non-contact sports there can be serious industrial injuries. Jockey Club statistics show that a rider can expect a fall every fourteen rides over jumps and hurdles and an injury every eighty.[130] It is paradoxical that a professional sportsperson must be fit to pursue their occupation but injuries often occur simply because they are playing sport. All sportsmen, of course, have built-in obsolescence. Sport is a physical activity and eventually experience no longer compensates for ageing bodies. Once the athletic peak is passed many find themselves on an inclined plane to obscurity. Some find it difficult to adjust to a life cut off from their previous mainline activity, an atypical lifestyle of training and competition. Few life experiences can offer the intensity and excitement of sporting competition and for some alcohol may replace this stimulation; for others drink might be part of self-mediation during the pain of the transition period. Michael Caulfield, Executive Manager of the Jockeys Association, has suggested that the real alcohol problem among jockeys emerges after their retirement when income, status and ego all decline.[131] Greaves says that his 'real drinking' started only after he quit League football and realised that at thirty-one he had done so prematurely and 'in my frustration at having let the good times go, I turned to the bottle'.[132] Hughie Gallacher, Scottish goal-scoring genius, also could not cope with leaving football, drank heavily, lost his wife, and eventually, in 1957, when facing an assault charge, threw himself under a train. [133] Cricketer John Sullivan, a Lancashire player in the early 1970s, 'couldn't accept that part of my life was over' and took to heavy drinking.[134] A century before, alcoholism took its toll on several Victorian cricketers when they retired including William Barnes, J.T. Brown, Tom Emmett, William Lockwood and Bobby Peel.[135] One of the most tragic examples of this syndrome was former world flyweight boxing champion Benny Lynch, who, before his drink-related death in 1946, was known to invite Glaswegian pub customers to punch him in the face for the price of a drink.[136] Nevertheless it must be stressed that in these and other cases it is not clear what can be attributed to sport and what to the personality of the individuals concerned.

Although ardent supporters – such as Nestor writing in *Scottish Sport* in May 1893 – feared for the future of both rugby and football if drinking by players dissuaded fathers from encouraging their sons to play the games, others, such as Montague Sherman, argued that rigid rules need not be imposed on sportsmen as unless they had the self-discipline with regard to diet and drink, they 'will never be any account as an athlete'.[137] Nevertheless most clubs and authorities believed that another form of discipline was required.

Although both William MacGregor, the founder of the Football League, and C.E. Sutcliffe, the Football League Secretary, were committed teetotallers, the issue of drinking by football players was generally left to the individual clubs.[138] Here there were other influential teetotallers at work including Sheffield Wednesday's Chairman, Charles Clegg; Arnold Hills, who created the Thames Ironworks team, which later became West Ham United, and once offered to clear the club's debts if it picked only teetotallers in the team;[139] and Walter Hart of Small Heath (later Birmingham City) who became President of the Birmingham Temperance Society. It was perhaps a legacy of Hills that West Ham had a policy of holding wages in trust for any player the club felt had a drinking problem.[140] The Wednesday Committee, under Clegg's chairmanship, insisted that no Wednesday player could work or even live in a public house and indeed club captain, F.H. Crawshaw was dismissed when he became a publican.[141] Sheffield Wednesday also disciplined some of its players for excessive drinking which had adversely affected their match performance; and when one of them was also found guilty in the magistrate's court of drunk and disorderly behaviour the club imposed a month's suspension and shortly afterwards put him on the transfer list.[142]

Most clubs, however, had links with the alcohol trade, but they too adopted a crime and punishment approach with fines and suspensions being used as deterrents. Aston Villa's board employed a private investigator to look into allegations of drunkenness and associated misconduct by the club's players.[143] Heart of Midlothian, among others, disciplined several players for drunkenness while travelling or training.[144] This occurred in rugby too – Wakefield Trinity expelled two of its players for going out drinking the night before a shock defeat in the Yorkshire Cup semi-final.[145] Such disciplinary policies prevailed for many years. Nevertheless although clubs often set rules to regulate a player's off-field activities, apart from a late-night curfew these could be lax and leave much to a player's discretion.[146] Some managers even proffered 'fatherly advice', as when Bill Nicholson of Tottenham Hotspur had a quiet word with Jimmy Greaves after he had made a public exhibition of himself during the victory celebrations following a European Cup Winners' tie with Hajduk Split.[147] That Greaves chose not to listen led to him, and three West Ham colleagues, being fined, dropped and sent home in the full glare of publicity on a later trip to Blackpool after they broke curfew to go out drinking.[148] In more recent times Arsenal, for one, appear to have adopted a disciplinary approach tempered with sympathy when a problem became acute. Paul Merson was fined, suspended, and sent home from an overseas tour for his alcohol-related misbehaviour, though the club chairman claimed that the board never contemplated dismissing him. Finally when he sought treatment, the club stood by him, and continued to pay his wages while he was hospitalised.[149] In 1991 Aston Villa paid for Paul McGrath to enter a detoxification clinic.[150] Many managers, especially those who utilise drinking sessions for team bonding purposes, would adopt the philosophy of Ron Atkinson, who maintained that 'as long as an individual didn't betray his club with bad social behaviour because of drink, and always performed to his potential on match day, then limited quantities of liquor at the appropriate time were acceptable'.[151] Pat Nevin argues that 'a good manager will know where to draw the line. He will know when it is useful and when it is destructive.'[152] Clubs have attempted to combat post-match drinking by allowing it to take place under supervision and most clubs now have a 'players bar'. This surprised at least one of the foreign imports to the English game whose experiences in Italy, Spain and Portugal were that post-game alcohol was frowned upon as being dehydrating.[153] Nevertheless there has been a degree of tolerance, even encouragement, of drinking within certain parameters. This, like the attitude of some managers towards alcohol and team bonding, can lead to a drinking culture. Nevertheless it is now less likely that the situations recalled by both Merson and Greaves will replicate themselves: on signing for Brentford the former felt he had joined 'a pub team', one in which the booze flowed free on the team coach, and both Spurs and West Ham had hard-drinking schools when the latter played there.[154]

At the international rather than the club level, after some observers claimed that James Cowan, captain and centre half of Scotland, had played against England when inebriated, he was never chosen again by the national selectors. One Scottish committee member maintained that 'after Cowan, we shall see that teams are under the care of the trainer from the Friday until the match'.[155] However, by the 1960s even the England manager, strict disciplinarian Alf Ramsay, was prepared to allow his squad to drink providing that it was in the team's hotel.[156]

All the domestic Football Associations have always had a 'bringing the game into disrepute' clause, though this has generally been aimed at players who open their mouths to criticise referees rather than to imbibe. In recent years, although the English lead body has taken a firm line against drug offenders, it has adopted a less severe position in respect of alcohol abusers especially where that has been due to diagnosed alcoholism. It has recognised that alcoholism is a disease rather than a moral failing. Paul Merson, who publicly confessed his addiction to alcohol and drugs, was treated leniently by the Football Association who ordered him to spend six weeks in a rehabilitation clinic but imposed no other punishment.[157] Some people regarded this as a soft line, but, as the Association's media officer pointed out, it acknowledged that drinking on this scale was an illness and 'players are human beings with real feelings'.[158] In the 1990s random drug testing has been introduced in football, along with many other sports, but the target has been performance-enhancing and recreational drugs not alcohol. Indeed today authorities and clubs seem to regard alcohol in a different light from other drugs, punishing consumption of the latter far more stringently. That the former is legally available – at least for over 18s – may account for the difference.

Attitudes and behaviours can be changed – otherwise the advertising industry would not exist – and football players are now also helping themselves avoid the perils of alcohol, or, more accurately, their union is doing it on their behalf. Although till recently the PFA has never focussed on the issue of alcohol abuse, it has always been prepared to help players if they have needed to go into clinics or hospitals to try and rehabilitate.[159] England international,

Malcolm Macdonald, could not deal with post-football life and had treatment for alcoholism financed by the PFA (and also the League Managers' Association).[160] Recently, however, the Association has stepped in to try and change dressing-room culture, something that it felt had altered little from the 1970s.[161] At senior level the old pros still had the attitude that you could always sweat out last night's booze at training, and that 'the beginner is only too apt to be led by the old stagers' remained as true as in 1906 when the Union Secretary wrote the comment.[162] The opportunity to rectify the situation came with the establishment of academies for young players by most professional clubs. Finance has been obtained from Adidas to develop an educational programme that will coach players for life rather than just for football. The efficacy of the scheme has yet to be evaluated, but doubtless it will be aided by the comments of England manager, Sven Goran Eriksson, who has stated that 'if you play for England you don't need to drink wine or beer'.[163] Fortunately he has something to build upon, as there has already been an influence from the influx of foreign players in British Football with their more temperate habits.

In other sports players have lessened their intake of alcohol voluntarily. One impact of professionalism on rugby union has been for the elite player to abandon the membership norm of the amateur version of the sport and reduce alcohol consumption to a level deemed consistent with professional playing performance.[164] Duncan Stewart cites Dean Richards, international forward and now coach of Leicester Tigers, who notes that training is not a 'social gathering' anymore.[165] Brian Ashton, at the time Irish national coach, commented that 'there has been quite a dramatic change to the extent where players at the top now either only drink on one occasion per week, probably a Saturday after the game, or in fact some of them now don't drink at all'.[166] In the mid-1980s the Scottish brewers McEwans would put a barrel of their product in the Scottish changing room. Nowadays, according to Scott Hastings, the Scottish centre, two hours must elapse before the players will consider having a drink.[167] It is ironic that the money brought into sport by sponsorship from the alcohol industry may have resulted in a more responsible attitude to drinking by sportspersons who have become more 'professional'. Although Tom Crisp, a doctor for a county cricket team, noted that '. . . a large proportion of first class cricketers are drinking alcohol every night',[168] in cricket too, there has been a decline in drinking after the game and many players stick to non-alcoholic drinks.[169]

Professional sportspersons are in a difficult position regarding their use of alcohol. They know that it might adversely affect their performance, yet they are encouraged to drink and promote their sponsor's products and generally find their employers are tolerant of a drinking culture, a continuation into professional ranks of a long-established amateur tradition.[170] The sports authorities and club officials face a dilemma. Unless the use of alcohol (and other recreational drugs) has enhanced sporting performance, they cannot imply that cheating occurred and thus apply sanctions to the athlete concerned. Any punishment is thus based on moral disapproval rather than legal logic.

Of course for some sportspersons the alcohol industry has offered long-term career prospects. Boxers, footballers and rugby players have for generations found a life after sport as landlords. This remains true even today: an analysis of data on 2,146 former soccer professionals, the earliest retiring from the game in the 1930s but the majority post the 1950s, shows the continuing importance of the alcohol trade in post-playing days. Of the cohort, 183 (8.5 per cent) took up jobs related to the drinks trade, the secondmost common occupation category after those related to football. The specific breakdown was pub landlords (130), bar owners/managers (15), brewery representatives (12), club owners/managers (9), hotel owners (9), restaurant owners (6) and off-licence owners (2).[171]

Other sportsmen have been used in an attempt to encourage sensible drinking by young men. The Army has used sports stars – such as rehabilitated alcoholic, Tony Adams, and Scottish rugby captain and military medic, Andy Wainwright – in videos shown in military base cinemas to promote sensible drinking. Backed by the Football Association, the Scottish Football Association, the Premier leagues north and south of the border, and supporters groups, the Portland Group, the education arm of the alcohol industry, have used ex-footballers turned television personalities – John Barnes and Alan Hansen in Scotland and Gary Lineker and Graeme Le Saux in England – as part of the 'I'll be Des' campaign which was designed to persuade drinkers to appoint a designated driver for their nights out. Football, and sport as a whole, is seen as a medium for gaining access to young men with the message rather than it being considered as a specific problem area.[172]

The use of sports stars in such a way demonstrates how the relationship between alcohol and sporting performance has changed over the past century. Traditionally, alcohol was always seen as an aid to strength, stamina and courage. But today, apart from a few sports that require a steady hand for aiming, such as shooting or archery, alcohol is no longer regarded as a performance-enhancing drug. Indeed, concern now centres on how drinking by sportspersons affects their non-sporting behaviour. Alcohol consumption in sport has now become a social rather than a sporting issue.

Notes

1. Barclay did not invent the training techniques but his success did a great deal to systematise it. His views on alcohol in training came from Sir John Sinclair's *Code of Health and Longevity*, London, 1807. Information supplied by Professor Peter Radford.

2. An Operator, *Selections From The Fancy*, Boston: Imprint Society, 1972, pp. 78–82.

3. Adrian N. Harvey, 'The Evolution of British Sporting Culture 1793–1850', unpublished D. Phil., Oxford University, 1995, pp. 276–7.

4. Vincent Dowling, *Fistiana, or Oracle of the Ring*, London, 1868, p. 143. We are indebted to Professor Peter Radford for this quote.

5. Fred Henning, *Fights for the Championship*, London, 1906, vol. 2, p. 161. Again we thank Professor Radford.

6. *Edinburgh Advertiser*, 9–13 November 1804.

7. *Say's Weekly Journal*, 6 October 1787.

8. *Edinburgh Advertiser*, 9–13 November 1804.

9. Brian Harrison, *Drink and the Victorians*, Keele, 1994, pp. 38–40.

10. Alan G. Foster, 'A Ghastly Performance', *The Leaflet*, July 1968, p. 54.

11. Barrie Houlihan, *Dying to Win*, Strasbourg, 1999, p. 34.

12. Robert Stainback, *Alcohol and Sport*, Champaign, Illinois, 1997, p. 63 citing historical research by others.

13. A.G. Steel and R.H. Lyttelton, *Cricket*, London, 1893, pp. 212–13.

14. W.F. Mandle, 'The Professional Cricketer in England in the Nineteenth Century', *Labour History*, 1972, XXIII, pp. 13–14. It should be noted that the Peel story may well be apocryphal.

15. Montague Shearman, *Athletics and Football*, London, 1888, pp. 171–4.

16. *Scottish Athletic Journal*, 13 October 1882.

17. John Weir, *Drink, Religion and Scottish Football 1873–1900*, Renfrew, 1992.

18. Medicus, 'Football From a Medical Point of View', *Scottish Football Annual* 1889/90, pp. 27–32.

19. R.C. Lehman, *Rowing*, London, 1898, pp. 115–17.

20. Fred Root, *A Cricket Pro's Lot*, London, 1937, p. 176.

21. *Scottish Athletic Journal*, 1 December 1885.

22. *Licensed Trade News*, 27 August 1910.

23. Jim Davies, *The Book of Guinness Advertising*, London, 1998, pp. 7 and 16.

24. Viscount Knebworth, *Boxing*, London,, 1931, p. 194.

25. Alphonse Abrahams in *The Practitioner*, quoted in *The British Deaf Sportsman* vol. 6, no. 1 April– June 1935. We are grateful to Julie Anderson for this reference.

26. J.G.P. Williams, *Medical Aspects of Sport and Physical Fitness*, Oxford, 1965, p. 82.

27. Houlihan, *Dying to Win*, p. 78.

28. For a full discussion see Stainback, *Alcohol and Sport*, pp. 49–63 and Thomas Reilly, 'Alcohol, Anti- Anxiety Drugs and Sport', in David R. Mottram, *Drugs in Sport*, London, 1996, pp. 144–72.
29. See Stainback, *Alcohol and Sport*, pp. 49–63.
30. Ibid., p. 49.
31. Thomas Reilly, 'Alcohol, Anti-Anxiety Drugs and Sport', p. 151; Houlihan, *Dying to Win*, p. 79.
32. Simon Hughes, professional cricketer, quoted in Duncan Stewart, 'Alcohol, the Ethical Dilemma', unpublished MA thesis, University of Warwick, 1997, p. 33.
33. Jimmy Greaves, *This One's On Me*, Newton Abbot, 1979, p. 10.
34. Quoted in Stewart, 'Alcohol, the Ethical Dilemma', p. 49.
35. Ibid., p. 34.
36. 'Real Lives: Jan Molby', *Total Sport*, 47 November 1999, p. 28.
37. Ron Atkinson, *Big Ron: A Different Ball Game*, London, 1998, p. 95.
38. Ibid., pp. 52–3.
39. Stewart, 'Alcohol, the Ethical Dilemma', p. 93.
40. *Guardian*, 21 February 1997.
41. *Rugby League Week (Sydney)*, 16 June 1999, p. 6.
42. Reilly, 'Alcohol, Anti-Anxiety Drugs and Sport', p. 147; Stewart, 'Alcohol, the Ethical Dilemma', p. 73.
43. Peter Arnold, *Darts*, London, 1984, p. 66.
44. *The Times*, 30 December 1974.
45. Quoted in Stewart, 'Alcohol, the Ethical Dilemma', p. 46.
46. Reilly, 'Alcohol, Anti-Anxiety Drugs and Sport', p. 156.
47. Ibid., p. 158.
48. Ibid., p. 155.
49. Mark Johnston, racehorse trainer, Radio 5, 4 June 1998.
50. Michael Tanner and Gerry Cranham, *Great Jockeys of the Flat*, Enfield, 1992, p. 46.
51. John Welcome, *Fred Archer: A Complete Study*, London, 1990, p. 29.
52. Lester Piggott, *Lester*, London, 1995, pp. 16 and 38.
53. Steve Wootton, *Nutrition For Sport*, London, 1989, p. 113.
54. *Archery U.K.*, Winter 1998, p. 9.
55. Jonjo O'Neill & Tim Richards, *Jonjo*, London, 1988, p. 94.
56. The Jockey Club, *Protocol and Rules for the Testing of Riders for Banned Substances*, London, August 1994.
57. Stewart, 'Alcohol, the Ethical Dilemma', p. 29.
58. See comments of Dr Gordon Morse of Cloud House, a Wiltshire residential addiction center, *Daily Telegraph*, 13 October 1998.
59. 'Stonehenge', *Manual of British Rural Sports*, London, 1857, p. 445.
60. Ken Thornett (with Tom Easton), *Tackling Rugby*, Melbourne, 1965, p. 121.
61. Greaves, *This One's On Me*, p. 77.
62. Paul Merson (with Harry Harris), *Rock Bottom*, Bloomsbury, 1995, p. 37; Denis Campbell, Pete May and Andrew Shields, *The Lad Done Bad*, Harmondsworth, 1996, p. 17.

63. Stainback, *Alcohol and Sport,* p. 67.

64. Wootton, *Nutrition For Sport,* p. 159.

65. Joyce Kay, 'From Coarse to Course: The First Fifty Years of the Royal Caledonian Hunt, 1777–1826', *Review of Scottish Culture,* 13, 2000/2001, pp. 30–9.

66. On the Scottish football situation see Weir, *Drink, Religion and Scottish Football.*

67. Cited in Ibid., footnote 15.

68. *Scottish Sport,* 4 September 1893 quoted in Ibid., footnote 23.

69. Root, *A Cricket Pro's Lot,* p. 23.

70. Stewart, 'Alcohol, the Ethical Dilemma', p. 13.

71. *Goring and Streatley Golf Club: The First Hundred Years 1895–1995,* Goring, 1995, p. 109.

72. See Pete May, *Sunday Muddy Sunday,* London, 1998.

73. *Independent on Sunday,* 1 July 1999.

74. Reilly, *Alcohol, Anti-Anxiety Drugs and Sport,* p. 153.

75. For example Don Mosey, *The Alderman's Tale,* London, 1991, p. 67; Rob Steen, 'Drinker's Guide to the Rugby World Cup', *Inside Sport,* 94, October 1999, pp. 28–9.

76. Alison Carle and John Nauright, 'Crossing the Line: Women Playing Rugby Union' in Timothy J.L. Chandler and John Nauright, *Making the Rugby World,* London, 1999, pp. 128–48.

77. Pete Davies, *I Lost My Heart to the Belles,* London, 1997.

78. For surveys see Russ Williams, *Football Babylon,* London, 1990; Campbell, May and Shields, *The Lad Done Bad*; and Andrew Shields, 'Some People are on the Piss', *Total Sport,* December 1996, pp. 94–102.

79. *Scottish Athletic Journal,* 30 March 1883. Cited in Weir, *Drink, Religion and Scottish Football.*

80. *North British Daily Mail,* 22 January 1878.

81. *Scottish Athletic Journal,* 26 August 1885.

82. *Scottish Sport,* 8 April 1898.

83. *Minutes of Heart of Midlothian F.C.,* 28 November 1902.

84. *Weekly News,* 24 April 1909.

85. *Temperance Herald,* February 1909.

86. *Golf Illustrated,* 7 July 1911.

87. Gerald Watts, *Royal St Georges,* Sandwich, 1996, p. 201.

88. W.I. Bassett, 'The Day's Work' in *The Book of Football,* London, 1906, pp. 110–13.

89. *Observer,* 6 September 1998.

90. Atkinson, *Big Ron: A Different Ball Game,* pp. 94 and 97.

91. *Independent on Sunday,* 10 September 1995.

92. *Daily Telegraph,* 13 October 1998.

93. *Minutes of Lancashire C.C.C.,* 31 January 1890; *Minutes of Leicester C.C.C.,* 11 June 1894.

94. *Cricket,* IX, 1890, p. 93; Leslie Duckworth, *The Story of Warwickshire Cricket,* London, 1974, p. 49.

95. We are grateful to John Harding, PFA historian, for these references.

96. Greaves, *This One's On Me*, p. 2.

97. Tony Adams (with Ian Ridley), *Addicted*, St Helens, 1998; Merson, *Rock Bottom*.

98. *Daily Telegraph*, 13 October 1998.

99. John Ford, *Boxiana,* Folio Society, 1976 edition, p. 85.

100. Wray Vamplew, *The Turf,* London, 1976, p. 164.

101. For allegations of alcoholism see Roger Mortimer, Richard Onslow and Peter Willett, *Biographical Encyclopedia of British Flat Racing*, London, 1978, pp. 174 and 219; Frances Collingwood, 'The Tragedy of Thomas Loates', *The British Racehorse* , October 1967, pp. 427–8.

102. Patricia Smyly, *Encyclopaedia of Steeplechasing*, London, 1979, p. 28.

103. Wray Vamplew, 'Still Crazy After All Those Years: Continuity in a Changing Labour Market for Professional Jockeys', *British Journal of Contemporary History,* 14.2, Summer 2000, p. 144.

104. Tony Rushmer, 'Cue Jimmy', *Total Sport,* April 1999, pp. 57–61.

105. Stewart, 'Alcohol, the Ethical Dilemma', p. 10.

106. *New Scientist,* 27 November 1999, pp. 5 and 36.

107. *Daily Telegraph*, 23 November 1998.

108. *Daily Telegraph*, 21 March 1997.

109. Merson, *Rock Bottom*, p. 2.

110. *New Scientist,* 27 November 1999, pp. 39–43.

111. Limited American data on the incidence of alcohol abuse and dependence among athletes suggest that the frequency of these problems approximates and may exceed general population estimates. Stainback, *Alcohol and Sport*, p. 72.

112. Martin Roderick, Ivan Waddington and Graham Parker, 'Playing Hurt: Managing Injuries in English Professional Football', *International Review of Sports Sociology,* 35.2, June 2000, pp. 165–80.

113. Peter Roebuck, *It Never Rains. . . A Cricketer's Lot*, London, 1984.

114. Jocelyn Targett, 'Slim Chance', *Sunday Telegraph Magazine*, 29 November 1998.

115. Frankie Dettori, *A Year In the Life of Frankie Dettori*, London, 1997, p. 2.

116. Quoted in Alan Lee, *Jump Jockeys*, London, 1989, p. 51.

117. Vamplew, 'Still Crazy', p. 144.

118. For an account of such pressures across a range of elite sports see Angela Patmore, *Sportsmen Under Stress*, London, 1986. For an historical view see Wray Vamplew, *Pay Up and Play the Game*, Cambridge, 1988, pp. 217–32.

119. Greaves, *This One's On Me*, p. 5.

120. Ibid., p. 10.

121. Merson, *Rock Bottom*, p. 28.

122. Quoted in Stewart, 'Alcohol, the Ethical Dilemma', p. 46.

123. Ibid., p. 76.

124. David Frith, *By His Own Hand: A Study of Cricket's Suicides*, London, 1991.

125. *Minutes of Football League*, 18 December 1891.
126. Root, *A Cricket Pro's Lot*, p. 170.
127. Vamplew, 'Still Crazy', p. 115.
128. Percy M. Young, *Bolton Wanderers*, London, 1961, p. 61; *Minutes of Lancashire C.C.C.*, 19 July 1912.
129. Vamplew, *Pay Up*, pp. 211–13.
130. Based on information supplied by Jockey Club Chief Medical Officer, Dr Michael Turner. A further breakdown suggests a fall every eight mounts over fences and every twenty-seven over hurdles.
131. Interview, 2 June 1999.
132. Greaves, *This One's On Me*, p. 5.
133. Tony Rennick, 'Hard Times' in Richard Cox, Dave Russell and Wray Vamplew, *Encyclopedia of British Football*, London, forthcoming.
134. Frith, *By His Own Hand*, p. 8
135. Keith Sandiford, *Cricket and the Victorians*, Aldershot, 1994, p. 104.
136. Rudolph Kenna and Ian Sutherland, *The Bevvy. The Story of Glasgow and Drink*, Glasgow, 2000, p. 88.
137. Nestor cited in Weir, *Drink, Religion and Scottish Football*; Montague Shearman, *Athletics and Football*, London, 1888, p. 173.
138. It would seem, however, that Sutcliffe used his position as editor of the *Athletic News* to restrict the advertising of alcohol in that journal.
139. *Licensing World and Licensed Trade Review*, 21 April 1900.
140. Charles Korr, 'West Ham United Football Club and the Beginnings of Professional Football in East London, 1895–1914', *Journal of Contemporary History*, XIII, 1978, p. 230.
141. *Minutes of Sheffield Wednesday F.C.*, 5 October 1898 and 19 February 1908.
142. *Minutes of Sheffield Wednesday F.C.*, 23 February 1898, 5 February and 2 April 1902.
143. Matthew Taylor, "Proud Preston': A History of the Football League, 1900–1939', unpublished PhD, De Montfort University, 1997, p. 208.
144. *Minutes of Heart of Midlothian F.C.*, 21 October, 1895 and 19 November 1910.
145. *Yorkshire Post*, 25 April 1889.
146. John Moynihan, *The Soccer Syndrome*, London, 1966, pp. 139–41. Interview with Archie Andrews, left half for Crystal Palace and Queen's Park Rangers in the 1950s.
147. Greaves, *This One's On Me*, p. 48.
148. Ibid., p. 69.
149. Merson, *Rock Bottom*, pp. 32, 37, 44, 84–5.
150. Campbell, May and Shields, *The Lad Done Bad*, p. 141.
151. Atkinson, *Big Ron: A Different Ball Game*, p. 95.
152. Quoted in Stewart, 'Alcohol, the Ethical Dilemma', p. 50.
153. 'Foreign Footballers', *Total Sport* 46, October 1999, p. 19.
154. Merson, *Rock Bottom*, p. 29; Greaves, *This One's On Me*, p. 69.

155. Weir, *Drink, Religion and Scottish Football,* note 60.
156. Greaves, *This One's On Me*, p. 50.
157. *Guardian*, 19 September and 1 November 1996.
158. 'My Sporting Life: Clare Tomlinson', *Total Sport*, March 1999, p. 36.
159. Letter from Gordon Taylor, Chief Executive PFA, 15 March 1999.
160. *Sunday Telegraph*, 11 October 1998.
161. Interview with Micky Burns, PFA, 5 May 1999.
162. John Cameron in *Spaldings Football Guide* 1906.
163. *Daily Telegraph*, 5 February 2001.
164. Stewart, 'Alcohol, the Ethical Dilemma', pp. 38–45.
165. Ibid., p. 106.
166. Ibid., p. 58.
167. Radio 5, 4 June 1998.
168. Interview in Stewart, 'Alcohol, the Ethical Dilemma', p. 124.
169. Simon Hughes in ibid. p. 39.
170. Paul Weaver, 'Slaves to the Corporate Rhythm', *Guardian*, 27 July 1999.
171. Andy Pringle and Neil Fissler *Where Are They Now?* London, 1996.
172. *Marketing Week*, 14 October 1999.

Conclusion: More than Beer and Skittles?

The seeming contradiction between the healthy lifestyle offered by participation in sport and the dangers to mind and body inherent in alcohol have led many to question the link between the two: is there an alternative to the symbiotic relationship between sport and alcohol?

Certainly during the last quarter of the nineteenth century significant sections of the temperance movement sought to provide an alternative, non-alcoholic culture for sport. This represented a significant change to the movement's traditional view of sport, which had expressed interest only in so far as sport could be used to demonstrate the degrading nature of the drink system. Cruel animal sports, violent folk football and sports involving gambling were viewed as part of the same continuum occupied by drunkenness and vice. The close association of sports with drinking, the idea that the rotund stomach of the copious beer-drinker was a sign of health and strength, and the lax morals associated with sporting events such as fairs and race meetings give the reformer more than enough reason to oppose involvement in sport.

But by the 1870s the new codes of football, shorn of the taint of the mob as a result of their codification by the public schools, and the game of cricket, rapidly discarding its overt links with gambling, had themselves taken on a moral element. The idea of 'a healthy body in a healthy mind' echoed much of temperance propaganda and the Muscular Christian belief that sport built character, held by many of the leaders of these sports, meant that these games appeared to share many of the imperatives of the temperance movement. Whereas the Rational Recreation movements of the mid-nineteenth century had failed to convince many working people that uplifting leisure pursuits were attractive in themselves, the explosion in the popularity of football from the late 1870s appeared to offer the possibility of linking a moral message to a recreation with mass appeal. Football and cricket were therefore enthusiastically embraced by the Church of England and, to a lesser extent, non-conformists in the north of England.

In particular, it was men from a Methodist, teetotal background, with its emphasis on self-improvement and moral purpose, who provided much of the drive which established soccer in its Lancashire and Midlands heartland and founded the Football League in 1888. It would be a mistake to overemphasise the importance of temperance campaigners to soccer as publicans and brewery employees also played leading roles both in clubs and the League and drinking and non-drinking administrators alike seemed to mix without rancour, as least as far as the temperance issue was concerned. Nevertheless, as Matt Taylor points out, 'the overwhelming tone of non-conformity on the [Football League] Committee seems to have been reflected in attitudes to drink and gambling'.[1] Birmingham's William MacGregor, the dominating influence in the early years of the Football League was a committed teetotaller; Charles Sutcliffe, the Football League's founding secretary, was a Sunday school preacher and ardent teetotaller; Charles Clegg of Sheffield and Walter Hart of Small Heath in Birmingham were both leading figures in the League and active temperance reformers; and John Lewis, the League's leading referee, was known as 'a fearless advocate of teetotalism' inclined to impromptu lectures on the liquid demon.[2] In Scotland, the Scottish Football Association was actually founded in 1873 at Dewar's Temperance Hotel in Glasgow, and Edinburgh protestant temperance campaigner John Hope sought to steer football in the city down the temperance route. Both Celtic and Hibernian also had early links with the Catholic temperance organisation the League of the Cross, although these links were somewhat short-lived.

Rugby's leaders, although generally coming from more orthodox Anglican backgrounds, also felt that their sport had a responsibility to give a moral lead: Fletcher Robinson argued that 'perhaps the best feature of this enthusiasm for Rugby football which has grown up among working men is the delight in hard exercise and consequent self-denial that it has taught him. A man cannot spend his nights and his wages in the public house if twice a week he has to face a hard struggle of forty minutes "each way".' In 1887 the Yorkshire Church Temperance Challenge Shield competition was started in order 'to promote an interest in football among the younger churchmen of Yorkshire and, secondly, to keep them out of the public houses'.[3]

Such sentiments did find some response among sportsmen. Local church and Sunday school leagues were formed as alternatives to pub-based clubs and leagues, and in some places actually outnumbered their drink-based rivals. Coffee houses also attempted to emulate licensed houses by setting up football and cricket teams, although without conspicuous success, and through the provision of facilities such as billiard tables.[4] By the turn of the century, the more sports-minded of the temperance campaigners were advocating tee-totalism as an essential attribute of the successful athlete. In 1892, the president of Batley rugby club blamed a poor cup run on his side's drinking habits, telling its annual general meeting that 'neither whisky nor ale will win a cup tie. Physical training required abstention from excess both in food and drink, and if this is not carried out there is no chance of going on to victory.' Successful teetotal athletes were highlighted as examples of the benefits of abstinence – in 1910 the world record break of Australian billiards player George Gray was ascribed to the fact that he was a non-smoker and a tee-totaller. The *Temperance Herald* scoured the world for such stories, even to the extent of reporting a walking race held in Germany won by a teetotaller in which, it noted darkly, thirty of the fifty-nine non-teetotal competitors failed to finish.[5] These assertions were not allowed to pass by the press of the drinks trade, which rarely missed the opportunity to put the case for the beneficial effects of its products; the Birmingham-based *Licensed Trade News* responded to the claims of the abstainers by arguing that

> The whole field of physical culture is filled with the best of men doing the best of work on alcohol in moderation and smoking with similar self-control . . . There is nothing to come near a good sound wholesome glass of beer as a thirst quencher, a dietetic, a support and a stimulant.[6]

Perhaps the most serious attempt to introduce temperance principles into professional sport was that of West Ham United founder Arnold Hills. As the owner of Thames Ironworks he had organised the club to provide recreation for his employees. He was also a militant advocate of the temperance cause. Under his leadership the club had introduced a system of fines for drinking and probation for players with alcohol-related problems. In 1901, following the club's incorporation as a limited company and the severing of its links with the Ironworks, he offered to pay off the club's not inconsiderable debts on one condition: that all the club's players become teetotallers. *The Licensing World*, another organ ever keen to expose the perfidy of the temperance movement, declared this to be 'one of the most impudent attempts ever made to propagate the milk and water doctrine . . . This is offering a premium on hypocrisy with a vengeance . . . the Thames Ironworks F.C. had far better remain in debt rather than accede to it.' A compromise was reached but the club continued to take a vigorously intrusive attitude towards its players' drinking habits, despite the fact that its first manager, Syd King, was a well-known alcoholic who would send young players out to buy beer for him.[7] Similar policies were adopted by the directors of Sheffield United, who in 1924 sacked Harold Gough from their playing staff after he had taken over the tenancy of a pub. His career was nearing its end and he had sought to secure his future with a pub tenancy, but such was the directors' commitment to temperance principles that they even tried to force him to pay back the wages he had received from the club since he became a landlord.[8]

In these moves to impose their principles on the sport, Hills and the Sheffield United directors were unusual among soccer's teetotal administrators. Most made little attempt to proselytise for their cause within the game, save to warn against excess. The fact that temperance advocates sat side by side with publicans and brewers on the sport's governing bodies, and even held committee meetings in public houses, demonstrated their ability to live and let live when it came to the needs of their sport. Their attitude was probably leavened by practical knowledge of the importance of drink to those who played and watched the game, together with a recognition that to force the issue would inevitably lead to conflict and a diminution of their influence. Other sporting bodies were also not keen to be closely identified with temperance issues; in 1931 the Professional Golfers' Association declined an offer to sponsor a trophy for the best score made by a total abstainer in the Assistants' Championship on the grounds that 'whilst advocating temperance the Association could not allow its name to be used in connection with total abstinence or other similar objects'. In contrast, those who sought to impose their views were generally forced to admit defeat – the Anglican sponsors of rugby's Yorkshire Temperance Shield simply withdrew from the game in the 1890s after it became clear that not only was the competition ineffective in promoting abstinence but that the trophy itself was being routinely displayed in the winning teams' local pubs. There was also a significant section of the temperance movement which was completely opposed to any connection between sport and the drinks trade, which effectively meant opposition to the vast majority of sporting activities. Both Liverpool and Glasgow during the inter-war years had draconian by-laws forbidding the playing of any form of games in pubs, a stance which achieved little other than to antagonise pub-goers and, as was claimed by opponents, to increase levels of drunkenness. The temperance movement had neither the resources nor the internal cohesion to offer any serious alternative for sport to break its close association with alcohol and the most successful of its sporting supporters were those who, like the leaders of the Football League, accepted and worked within the prevailing sports culture.[9]

The chances for the severing of the link between drink and sport today are even more miniscule. The profound changes which the brewing industry has undergone in Britain since the 'Beer Orders' of 1989 – which sought to encourage competition among brewers by reducing the number of tied pubs they could own – have seen an increase in the industry's reliance on sport as a marketing vehicle. The Beer Orders led to profound changes in the industry, including the abandonment of brewing by names such as Whitbread and Bass, and resulted in the conversion of thousands of pubs into purely retail outlets. As the brewers divested themselves of pubs, new companies entered the field, rebranding pubs to suit those 'segments' of the population which marketing departments were targeting. Family pubs, yuppie bars, faux Irish music pubs and sports bars replaced the traditional pub in many city and town centres. 'Pubs are just like other High Street retailers . . . We want to be the Marks & Spencer of pub retailing,' said the founder of the J.D. Wetherspoon chain in 1995.[10] In one sense, these developments often helped to promote sport – the ubiquitous big screen TVs with satellite links for major sporting events are a powerful draw for pub customers and are often linked to themed pub or beer promotional activities: indeed, 'going down the pub for the big match' especially for high-profile football matches such as England or Scotland internationals seems to have become part of the ritual of identifying with and supporting national sports teams for many males in the 1990s. But the relationship of these pure retail pubs to their local communities is different from that of the more traditional pub. These new pubs seek to provide a 'leisure occasion', in the words of the marketers, rather than a fulcrum for community activity. The pub which served as a base for the local football, cricket, darts or angling team – not to mention a whole host of other activities – is dying out: such activities do not sufficiently increase turnover or profit levels.

This is not to suggest that there was ever a golden age of British pubs in which a happy community gathered together as one to cheer on their sporting representatives in an atmosphere of convivial warm beer. As we have seen, the process by which pubs are being transformed into retail outlets has its roots in the breweries' rush to acquire pubs in the late nineteenth century. Nor would it be correct to forget the poor state and lack of facilities of many pubs in the past. Nostalgia for an idealised past is an emotion shared both by sports fans and beer drinkers alike. Nevertheless, it is undeniable that the pub is less and less seen as a community centre and just another in a range of leisure activities. The fact that approximately 20,000 pubs have closed down in Britain since 1950 and that the average walking time from home to pub has increased from five to thirteen minutes is further evidence of the pub's decline as a local social centre.[11] Coupled with the decline of sport in state schools and a decrease in public park space available for sports, the changing nature of the pub may help to contribute to a decline in opportunities to play sports.

At the corporate level however, it seems likely that elite sports will only continue to prosper from their relationship with alcohol. Sport offers a unique avenue for the drinks industry to reach its most lucrative target audience of males aged between 16 and 35. The increasingly global nature of sports brands, whether belonging to competitions or clubs, makes them even more attractive to an industry which itself is consolidating across national boundaries into 'super-breweries', such as Belgium's Interbrew, making marketing and advertising campaigns simpler and cheaper. The development of such campaigns can be seen in Budweiser's 'Whassup?' campaign of 2000, which took the idea of global sport a step further by referring not to the actual sports being watched by the participants but to the common male culture of watching sport on TV. Ironically, these advertising campaigns owe much to the soft drinks brands like Coca Cola and Pepsi Cola, which led the way in global advertising campaigns in the late 1960s and 1970s. The growing importance of satellite TV in the financing of sport both lessens sport's dependency on alcohol-derived revenue yet increases its attractiveness as an advertising medium for the drinks industry.

Nevertheless, this does not mean to say that many of the traditional objections to the link between sport and alcohol have been lessened. The desire to escape the narrow confines of social class stereotyping means that sports viewed as predominately working class, such as football and rugby league, have long expressed a desire to shift their sponsorship away from 'booze and fags' companies. There also remains a significant body of opinion in public health circles that alcohol advertising should be treated in the same way as tobacco advertising – for example, in France the government has banned tobacco and alcohol advertising in sport. In 1999 the pressure group Alcohol Concern, supported by the British Medical Association, called for tight restrictions on alcohol advertising in sport in order to reduce the risk of children being exposed to drinking through its association with sports stars. Their call found little support, but recent government campaigns against 'yob culture' and the banning of drinking in public could lay the basis for a wider assault on alcohol's association with sport in the future, especially if there is a resurgence in football hooliganism.[12]

But even if the campaigners against alcohol prevailed and the drinks industry's marketing support for sport was severed, it would do little to undermine their long-term relationship. Although the link between sport and alcohol is highlighted most prominently today by multi-national breweries sponsoring multi-millionaire athletes, the connection is one which even the most severe regime of prohibition would struggle to eliminate. In short, the desire to relax with alcohol and amuse oneself with games is almost as old as human culture itself – and, many would argue, long may it continue.

Notes

1. Matthew Taylor, '"Proud Preston": A History of the Football League', unpublished PhD thesis, De Montfort University, 1997, p. 45. See also Simon Inglis, *League Football and the Men Who Made It*, London 1988.
2. C.E. Sutcliffe and F. Hargreaves, *History of the Lancashire Football Association*, Blackburn 1928, p. 18.
3. B. Fletcher Robinson, *Rugby Football*, London 1896, p. 49. *Yorkshire Post*, 5 December 1887.
4. For example, Jack Williams has discovered that in eight major towns in the north of England church teams outnumbered both teams based on pubs and workplaces between 1900 and 1939. Jack Williams, 'Churches, Sport and Identities in the North, 1900–1939' in Jeff Hill and Jack Williams (eds), *Sport and Identity in the North of England*, Keele, 1996, p. 120. On coffee houses, see Mark Girouard, *Victorian Pubs*, Yale, 1984, p. 203 and *Temperance Caterer* 15 January 1910.
5. *Yorkshire Post*, 28 April 1892; *Temperance Caterer*, 15 October 1910; *Temperance Herald*, September 1910.
6. *The Licensed Trade News*, 27 August 1910.
7. *Licensing World*, 21 April 1900. For the early history of West Ham, see Charles Korr, *West Ham United*, London 1986, pp. 1–16.
8. Dave Russell, *Football and the English*, Preston, 1997, p. 93.
9. Professional Golfers' Association, Minutes of the Quarterly Committee Meetings, 23 March and 13 April 1931. For the Temperance Shield, see Tony Collins, *Rugby's Great Split*, London 1998, p. 120. On Temperance opposition to pub games see Licensed Victuallers' Central Protection Society, *An Examination of the Evidence Before the Royal Commission on Licensing*, London, 1931, pp. 82–4, and Mass-Observation, *The Pub and the People*, London, 1943, pp. 304–8.
10. Quoted in Dominic Hobson, *The National Wealth*, London, 1999, p. 820.
11. Ibid., p. 824.
12. *Guardian*, 31 August 1999.

Bibliography

Archives

Advertising Standards Authority, London:
Materials related to sport in the advertising of alcohol.

Alcohol Concern, London:
Materials relating the use of alcohol in sport.

Bass Museum Archives, Burton on Trent:
Bass, Ratcliff & Gretton Ltd, Directors' minute books;
Worthington Board of Directors, minute books;
Henry Mitchell & Co Ltd Managing Directors Board Meetings minute books.

Brewers' And Licensed Retailers' Association, London:
Materials relating to advertising and sponsorship.

Calderdale Archives, Halifax:
Magistrates licensing records 1871–97.

Companies House, Cardiff:
Shareholder records of professional sports clubs.

Courage Archives, Bristol:
H & G Simonds Board of Directors minute books;
Truman's Board of Directors Meetings minute books.

Football League, Lytham St Annes:
Minutes.

Heart of Midlothian Football Club, Edinburgh:
Minutes.

Kirklees Archives, Huddersfield:
Records of Bentley & Shaw Limited, Lockwood.

Lancashire County Cricket Club, Old Trafford, Manchester:
Minutes.

Leicestershire County Cricket Club, Leicester:
Minutes.

Mass-Observation Archives, University of Sussex, Brighton:
Workstown Papers 1937–40 and 'Britain Revisited';
Pub Observations 1947–48;
Miscellaneous papers relating to Sport, Courage Breweries and Guinness.

Professional Golfers' Association Archives, The Belfry, Sutton Coldfield:
Minutes.

Rugby Football League, Leeds:
Council minute books.

Rugby Football Union, Twickenham:
Miscellaneous papers.

Scottish Brewing Archive, University of Glasgow:
Scottish Brewers Limited Board of Directors and Advertising Committee minutes.
William McEwan and Company Limited, Board of Directors minutes and Press
    Advertising books.
William Younger and Company Limited, Board of Directors minutes.

Sheffield Wednesday Football Club, Sheffield:
Minutes.

Tetley's Brewery Wharf Archives, Leeds:
Works Consultative Committee minute books;
Brewery Cricket Club minute books;
Business diaries.

West Yorkshire Archives, Leeds:
Papers relating to Joshua Tetley & Sons.

Newspapers and Magazines

The Anchor
Archery U.K.
Bell's Life In London
Birmingham Daily Post
Bridge of Allan Reporter

Bristol Evening Post
The British Deaf Sportsman
Caterer and Hotel Keeper
C.B. Fry's Magazine
Country Brewers' Gazette
Cricket
Cricketer
Daily Express
Daily Telegraph
Darts Weekly News
Deer's Leap
Deerstalker
Edinburgh Advertiser
Edinburgh Evening News
Football Players' Magazine
Glasgow Evening Times
Glasgow Herald
Golf Illustrated
Guardian
Independent on Sunday
Inside Sport
The Leaflet
Licensed Trade News
Licensed Victualler
Licensed Victualler's Mirror
Licensing World and Licensed Trade Review
London Evening News
Manchester Evening News
Manchester Guardian
Marketing Week
Monthly Bulletin
Morning Advertiser
National Guardian
New Scientist
North British Daily Mail
Northern Echo
Observer
Quoiting World
Roundabout
Rugby League Week (Sydney)
Rugby World
Say's Weekly Journal
The Scotsman

Scottish Athletic Journal
Scottish Sport
Scottish Wines, Spirits and Beer Trades Review
Stirling Journal
Stirling Observer
Sunday Telegraph
Temperance Bells
The Temperance Caterer
Temperance Herald
The Times
Toby Jug
Total Sport
Weekly News
Yorkshire Owl
Yorkshire Post

Published Books and Articles

Adams, Tony (with Ian Ridley), *Addicted*, St Helens, 1998.

Anon, *Lawful Games on Licensed Premises*, London, undated [c1900].

——, *A Short History of George Younger & Son Ltd., Alloa. 1762–1925*, Alloa 1925.

——, *Sports and Points Worth Considering*, Wakefield, 1937.

——, *Inns of Sport*, London, 1949.

——, *Your Club*, London, 1950.

——, *Superbrands*, London, 1998.

An Operator, *Selections From The Fancy*, Boston, Imprint Society Edition, 1972.

Arlott, John, *Krug. House of Champagne*, London, 1976.

Armstrong, Gary, and Young, Malcolm, 'Fanatical Football Chants: Creating and Controlling the Carnival' in *Culture, Sport, Society*, Volume 2 Number 3, Autumn 1999.

Arnold, A. J., *A Game That Would Pay*, London, 1988.

Arnold, Peter, *Darts*, London, Deans, 1984.

Ashplant T.G., 'London Working Men's Clubs, 1875–1914' in Eileen and Stephen Yeo (eds), *Popular Culture and Class Conflict 1590–1914*, Brighton, 1981.

Aspects of Culture and Recreation in 19th Century and Early 20th Century Huddersfield, Bretton Hall College, Urban Studies Series, no. 3, Summer 1979.

Atkinson, Ron, *Big Ron: A Different Ball Game*, London, Andre Deutsch, 1998.

Auty, T., Jenkins, J., and Pierce, D., *Who's Who of Welsh International Rugby Players*, Wrexham, 1991.

Backhouse, David, *Home Brewed. A History of Breweries and Public Houses in the Swindon Area*, Swindon, 1992.

Bailey, Peter, *Leisure and Class in Victorian England*, London, 1978.

——, 'Introduction: Making Sense of Music Hall' in Peter Bailey (ed.), *Music Hall, The Business of Pleasure*, Milton Keynes, 1986, p. x.

Barr, Andrew, *Drink: A Social History*, London 1998 (Pimlico Edition).

Barrett, Tom, *Darts*, Pan, 1973.

Bass Brewers, *Sponsorship: Mixing Business With Pleasure*, Burton, 1998.

Bassett, W.I., 'The Day's Work' in *The Book of Football*, London, 1906.

Belchem, John, *Industrialisation and the Working Class*, Aldershot, 1990.

Bently Capper, W. (ed.), *Licensed Houses and their Management*, London, 1923 .

Berrison, B., and Merrington, J.P., *The Centenary History of the Newcastle Breweries Ltd, 1890–1990*, Dunfermline, 1990.

Bills, Peter, *Passion in Exile. 100 Years of London Irish RFC*, Edinburgh, 1998.

Birley, Derek, *Sport and the Making of Britain*, Manchester, 1993.

——, *Land of Sport and Glory*, Manchester, 1993.

——, *A Social History of English Cricket*, London, 1999.

Boston, Richard, *Beer and Skittles*, London, 1976.

Brailsford, Dennis, *Bareknuckles: A Social History of Prizefighting*, Cambridge, 1988.

——, *British Sport – A Social History*, Cambridge, 1992.

Brander, Michael, *The Life and Sport of the Inn*, London, 1973.

Brewers' Association of Scotland, *Annual Reports*, Glasgow.

Brewers' Society, *Inn Signs: Their History and Meaning*, London, 1969.

British Market Research Bureau Ltd, *Licensed Premises. Report on an Attitude Survey*, London, August 1960.

Brown, Callum, 'Sport and the Scottish Office in the Twentieth Century: The Control of a Social Problem' in J.A. Mangan (Editor) *Sport in Europe: Politics, Class, Gender* London, 1999.

Burnett, John, *Liquid Pleasures: A Social History of Drinks in Modern Britain*, London 1999.

Campbell, Denis, May, Pete, and Shields, Andrew, *The Lad Done Bad*, Harmondsworth, 1996.

Carle, Alison, and John Nauright, John, 'Crossing the Line: Women Playing Rugby Union' in Timothy J.L. Chandler and John Nauright, *Making the Rugby World*, London, 1999.

Carnibella, Giovanni, Fox, Anne, Fox, Kate, McCann, Joe, Marsh, James and Marsh, Peter, *Football Violence in Europe. A Report to the Amsterdam Group*, MCM Research Ltd, Oxford, 1996.

Channon, Geoffrey, 'George's and Brewing in Bristol' in *Studies in the Business History of Bristol*, Bristol, 1988.

Chartres, John, 'Joshua Tetley & Son, 1890s to 1990s' in John Chartres and Katrina Honeyman (eds), *Leeds City Business*, Leeds, 1993.

Clapson, Mark, *A Bit Of A Flutter, Popular Gambling And English Society c1823–1961*, Manchester, 1992.

Collingwood, Francis, 'The Tragedy of Thomas Loates', *The British Racehorse* October 1967.

Collins, Tony, *Rugby's Great Split*, London, 1998.

Cousins, G., *Golf in Britain*, London, 1975.

Cox, Barrie, *English Inn and Tavern Names*, Nottingham, 1994.

Cox, Richard, Jarvie, Grant and Vamplew, Wray, (eds), *Encyclopedia of British Sport*, London, 2000.

——, Russell, Dave and Vamplew, Wray, (eds), *Encyclopedia of British Football*, Oxford, Helicon, 2001.

Craig, S., 'Fever Pitch, 1909', *History Today*, May 1999.

Crawford, S.A.G.M., 'Coursing' in *Encyclopedia of World Sport*, Oxford, 1996.

Crowds Committee, *Report of the Departmental Committee on Crowds*, London HMSO 1924, Cmd. 2088.

Crump, Jeremy, 'Provincial Music Hall: Promoters and Public in Leicester, 1863–1929' in Peter Bailey (ed.), *Music Hall, The Business of Pleasure*, Milton Keynes, 1986.

Curtis, H.L., *Principles of Training for Amateur Athletics*, London, 1892.

Dafydd, Myrddin ap, *Welsh Pub Names*, Llanrwst, 1991.

Davies, Andrew, 'Leisure in the "Classic Slum" 1900–1939' in Andrew Davies and Steven Fielding (eds), *Workers' Worlds: Cultures and Communities in Manchester and Salford 1880–1939*, Manchester, 1992.

Davies, Hunter, *The Glory Game*, London, 1972.

Davies, Jim, *The Book of Guinness Advertising*, London, 1998.

Davies, Pete, *I Lost My Heart to the Belles*, London, Mandarin, 1997.

Delaney, Trevor, *The Grounds of Rugby League*, Keighley, 1991.

Department of Education and Science, *Report of the Committee on Football*, London HMSO, 1968.

Department of the Environment, *Football Spectator Violence. Report of an Official Working Group*, London HMSO, 1984.

Dettori, Frankie, *A Year in the Life of Frankie Dettori*, London, Mandarin, 1997.

Dingle, A.E., 'Drink and Working Class Living Standards in Britain 1870–1914', *Economic History Review*, vol. 25, 1972

Donnachie, Ian, *A History of the Scottish Brewing Industry*, Glasgow, 1979.

Dowling, Vincent, *Fistiana, or Oracle of the Ring*, London, 1868.

Duckworth, Leslie, *The Story of Warwickshire Cricket*, London, 1974.

Dunkling, Leslie and Wright, Gordon, *A Dictionary of Pub Names*, London, 1987.

Dunning, Eric, Murphy, Patrick and Williams, John, *The Roots of Football Hooliganism*, London, 1988.

——, Murphy, Patrick and Williams, John, *Football On Trial*, London, 1990.

Eileen and Stephen Yeo (eds), *Popular Culture and Class Conflict 1590–1914*, Brighton, 1981.

Eley, P. and Riley, R.C., *Public Houses and Beerhouses in 19th Century Portsmouth*, Portsmouth, 1983.

——, and Riley, R. C., *The Demise of Demon Drink? Portsmouth Pubs 1900–1950*, Portsmouth, 1991.

Elkins, Ted, *Our Trade*, Shepton Mallet, 1978.

Escott, T.H.S., *England: Its People, Polity and Pursuits*, 2 vols, London, 1885.

Faulkner, N., *Allied Breweries: A Long Life*, Rochester, 1988.

Finn, Timothy, *Pub Games of England*, London, 1975.

Fishwick, Nicholas, *English Football and Society 1910–1950*, Manchester, 1989.

Flynn, Tony, *A History of the Pubs of Eccles*, Manchester, undated.

Football Crowd Behaviour: Report by a Working Group Appointed by the Secretary of State for Scotland, London HMSO, 1977.

Ford, John, *Boxiana*, London, Folio Society, 1976.

Forman, Charles, *Industrial Town: Self-Portrait of St Helens in the 1920s*, London, 1978.

Foster, Alan G., 'A Ghastly Performance', *The Leaflet*, July 1968.

Fox, Kate, 'Factors influencing good crowd behaviour: A case study of British Horse-racing' in *Australian Society for Sports History Bulletin*, no. 32, August 2000.

Frith, David, *By His Own Hand: A Study of Cricket's Suicides*, London, Stanley Paul, 1991.

Gaulton, A.N., *The Encyclopedia of Rugby League Football*, London, 1968.

Girouard, Mark, *Victorian Pubs*, Yale, 1984.

Glover, Brian, *Prince of Ales. The History of Brewing in Wales*, Stroud, 1993.

Godfrey, Christine, *Preventing Alcohol and Tobacco Problems*, vol. 1, London, 1990.

Golby, J.W. and Purdue, A.W., *The Civilisation of the Crowd, Popular Culture in England 1750–1900*, London, 1984.

Goring and Streatley Golf Club: The First Hundred Years 1895–1995, Goring, 1995.

Gourvish, T.R. and Wilson, R.G., 'Profitability in the Brewing Industry 1885–1914', *Business History*, vol. 27, 1985.

——, *Norfolk Beers from English Barley. A History of Steward & Paterson 1793–1963*, Norwich, 1987.

——, and Wilson, R.G., *The British Brewing Industry*, Cambridge, 1994.

Greaves, Jimmy, *This One's On Me*, Newton Abbott, Readers Union, 1979.

Guinness, Edward, *The Guinness Book of Guinness*, London, 1988.

Gutzke, David, *Protecting the Pub: Brewers and Publicans Against Temperance*, Suffolk, 1989.

Hamilton, Ian, *The Faber Book of Soccer*, London, 1992.

Harrison, Brian, 'Religion and Recreation in 19 Century England', *Past and Present*, 38, December 1967.

——, 'Pubs' in H.J. Dyos and M. Wolff (eds), *The Victorian City: Images and Realities*, vol. 1, London, 1973.

——, *Drink and the Victorians*, Second Edition, Keele, 1994.

Hawkins, K., *A History of Bass Charrington*, Oxford, 1978.

——, and Pass, C.L., *The Brewing Industry. A Study of Industrial Organisation and Public Policy*, London, 1979.

Haydon, Peter, *The English Pub*, London, 1994.

Henning, Fred, *Fights for the Championship*, London, 1906.

Hey, Valerie, *Patriarchy and Pub Culture*, London, 1986.

Hobson, Dominic, *The National Wealth*, London, 1999.

Holt, Richard, *Sport and the British*, Oxford, 1989.

Home Office Committee of Inquiry into Crowd Safety and Control at Sports Grounds, *Final Report* Cmnd. 9710, London HMSO, 1986.

Home Office, *The Hillsborough Stadium Disaster, Inquiry by the Right Hon Lord Justice Taylor, Final Report*, London HMSO, 1990 .

Hopcraft, Arthur, *The Football Man*, Second Edition, London, 1971.

Houlihan, Barrie, *Dying to Win*, Council of Europe, Strasbourg, 1999.

Huggins, Mike, *Flat Racing and British Society 1790–1914*, London, 1999.

Hull & District Rugby Football Union, *Official Guide 1895–96*, Hull, 1895.

Inglis, Simon, *The Football Grounds of Great Britain*, Second Edition, London, 1987.

——, *League Football and the Men Who Made It*, London, 1988.

Jackson, Michael, *The English Pub*, London, 1976.

Janes, Hurford, *The Red Barrel: A History of Watney Mann*, London, 1963.

Jennings, Paul, *The Public House in Bradford, 1770–1970*, Keele, 1995.

Jockey Club, *Protocol and Rules for the Testing of Riders for Banned Substances*, London, Jockey Club, 1994.

Jones, Michael, *Time, Gentlemen, Please! Early Brewery Posters in the Public Record Office*, London, 1997.

Kay, Joyce, 'From Coarse to Course: The First Fifty Years of the Royal Caledonian Hunt, 1777–1826', *Review of Scottish Culture*, 13, 2000/01.

Kellet, M.A., 'The Power of Princely Patronage: Pigeon-Shooting in Victorian Britain' *International Journal of the History of Sport*, Vol. 11, no. 1, April 1994.

Kenna, Rudolph, and Sutherland, Ian, *The Bevvy. The Story of Glasgow and Drink*, Glasgow, 2000.

Knebworth, Viscount, *Boxing*, London, Seeley, 1931.

Korr, Charles, 'West Ham United Football Club and the Beginnings of Professional Football in East London, 1895–1914', *Journal of Contemporary History*, XIII, 1978.

——, *West Ham United*, London, 1986

Lackey, Clifford, *Quality Pays . . . The Story of Joshua Tetley & Son*, Ascot, 1985.

Larwood, Jacob, and Camden Hotten, J., *English Inn Signs*, Exeter, 1986.

Lawton, Tommy, *My Twenty Years of Soccer*, London, 1955.

Lee, Alan, *Jump Jockeys*, London, Ward Lock, 1989.

Lehman, R.C., *Rowing*, London, Innes, 1898.

Licensed Victuallers' Central Protection Society, *An Examination of the Evidence Before the Royal Commission on Licensing*, London, 1931.

Lowerson, John, 'Angling' in Tony Mason (ed.), *Sport in Britain. A Social History*, Cambridge, 1989.

——, *Sport and the English Middle Classes, 1870–1914*, Manchester 1993.

Malcolm, Dominic, 'Cricket Spectator Disorder: Myths and Historical Evidence' in *The Sports Historian*, Number 19 (1) May 1999.

Mandle, W. F., 'The Professional Cricketer in England in the Nineteenth Century', *Labour History*, XXIII, 1972.

Marples, M., *A History of Football*, London, 1954.

Marsh, Peter, and Fox Kilby, Kate, *Drinking and Public Disorder*, London, 1992.

Marwick, Arthur, *The Deluge. British Society and the First World War*, Second Edition, London 1991.

Mason, Tony, *Association Football and English Society 1863–1915*, Brighton, 1980.

Mass-Observation, *Report on Juvenile Drinking*, Sheffield, 1943.

——, *The Pub and the People*, London, 1943.

Mathias, Peter, *The Brewing Industry in England, 1700–1830*, Cambridge, 1959.

Matthews, Stanley, *Feet First*, London, 1948.

May, Pete, *Sunday Muddy Sunday*, London, Virgin, 1998.

Mayle, Peter, *Thirsty Work – Ten Years of Heineken Advertising*, London, 1983.

McConville, Chris, 'Football, Liquor and Gambling in the 1920s' in *Sporting Traditions*, vol. 1, no. 1, November 1984.

McKibbin, Ross, *The Ideologies of Class*, Oxford, 1990.

Medicus, 'Football From a Medical Point of View', *Scottish Football Annual* 1889/90.

Merson, Paul (with Harris, Harry), *Rock Bottom*, London, Bloomsbury, 1995.

Metcalfe, Alan, 'Organised Sport in the Mining Communities of South Northumberland, 1880–1889', *Victorian Studies*, 25, Summer 1982.

Mitchells & Butlers, *Fifty Years of Brewing 1879–1929*, Birmingham, 1929.

Monckton, H.A., *A History of the English Public House*, London, 1969.

——, *The Story of the British Pub*, Sheffield, 1982.

Mortimer, R., Onslow, R., and Willett, P., *Biographical Encyclopedia of British Flat Racing*, London, 1978.

Mosey, Don, *The Alderman's Tale*, London, 1991.

Mott, James, 'Miners, Weavers and Pigeon Racing' in Michael A. Smith, Stanley Parker and Cyril S. Smith (eds), *Leisure and Society in Britain*, London, 1973.

Mottram, David R., *Drugs in Sport*, London, Spon, 1996.

Moynihan, John, *The Soccer Syndrome*, London, 1966.

Murphy, Alex, *Saints Hit Double Top*, London, 1967.

Murray, Bill, *The Old Firm. Sectarianism, Sport and Society in Scotland*, Edinburgh, 1984.

Murray, Francis, *The Open*, London, 2000.

Neville, Sidney O., *Seventy Rolling Years*, London, 1958.

Oddy, Derek J., and Miller, Derek S., (eds), *Diet and Health in Modern Britain*, London, 1985.

O'Neill, Jonjo and Richards, Tim, *Jonjo*, London, 1988.

Oxford English Dictionary, Second Edition on CD-Rom, Oxford, 1992.

Parry, Lewis J., *Freedom to Drink*, London, 1985.

Parry-Jones, David, 'Is Rugby on the Path of Soccer?' *Rugby World*, October 1980.

Patmore, Angela, *Sportsmen Under Pressure*, London, 1986.

Pearson, Geoffrey, *Hooligan: A History of Respectable Fears*, London, 1983.

Peebles, Ian, *The Watney Book of Test Match Grounds*, London, 1967.

Pepper, Barrie, *Old Inns and Pubs of Leeds*, Leeds, 1997.

Phillips, Tony, *Pubs of Tower Hamlets*, London, 1988.

Piggott, Lester, *Lester*, London, 1995.

Pringle, Andy and Fissler, Neil, *Where Are They Now?*, London, 1996.

Public Disorder and Sporting Events: Report of a Joint Sports Council/Social Science Research Council Panel, London, 1978.

Pudney, John, *A Draught of Contentment. The Story of the Courage Group*, London, 1971.

Raitt Kerr, Diana, *Hambledon Cricket and The Bat and Ball Inn*, Chichester, 1951.

Rennick, Tony, 'Hard Times' in Richard Cox, Dave Russell and Wray Vamplew, *Encyclopedia of British Football*, London, forthcoming.

Rennison, B., 'Not So Common, the Pub in the North East', *The Local Historian*, 1995, 25.

Report of the Royal Commission on Licensing (England and Wales) 1929–1931, London, 1932.

Report of the Royal Commission on Licensing (Scotland), Edinburgh, 1931.

Richards, Timothy M., and Curl, James Stevens, *City of London Pubs*, 1973.

Richardson, Neil, Gall, Alan and Wilson, Jeff, *Wigan's Pubs*, Manchester, undated.

Ripley, Mike, and Wood, Fiona, *'Beer is Best' The Collective Advertising of Beer 1933–1970*, London, 1994.

Ritchie, Berry, *An Uncommon Brewer. The Story of Whitbread 1742–1992*, London, 1992.

Roberts, Robert, *The Classic Slum*, Manchester, 1971.

Robinson, B.F., *Rugby Football*, London, 1896.

Roderick, Martin, Waddington, Ivan and Parker, Graham, 'Playing Hurt: Managing Injuries in English Professional Football', *International Review of Sports Sociology*, 35.2, June 2000.

Roebuck, Peter, *It Never Rains . . . A Cricketer's Lot*, London, 1984.

Root, Fred, *A Cricket Pro's Lot*, London, Edward Arnold, 1937.

Royal Commission On Licensing (England And Wales) 1929–31, *Report*, London, 1932.

Royal Commission on Liquor Licensing Laws, *Final Report*, London, 1899.

Russell, D., *Football and the English*, Preston, 1997.

Sandiford, Keith, *Cricket and the Victorians*, Aldershot, 1994.

Shearman, Montague, *Athletics and Football*, London, 1888.

Sinclair, Sir John, *Code of Health and Longevity*, London, 1807.

Sir Norman Chester Centre for Football Research, Football and Football Spectators after Hillsborough: A National Survey of Members of the Football Supporters' Association, Leicester, 1990.

Smith, Horatio, *Festivals, Games and Amusements*, London, 1831.

Smyly, Patricia, *Encyclopaedia of Steeplechasing*, London, 1979.

Stainback, Robert, *Alcohol and Sport*, Champaign, Illinois, 1997.

Steel, A.G. and Lyttelton, R.H., *Cricket*, London, 1893.

Stevenson, John, *British Society 1914–45*, London, 1984.

'Stonehenge', *Manual of British Rural Sports*, London, Routledge, 1857.

Sutcliffe, C.E., and Hargreaves, F., *History of the Lancashire Football Association*, Blackburn, 1928.

Swift, Frank, *Football in the Goalmouth*, London, 1948

Tanner, Michael and Cranham, Gerry, *Great Jockeys of the Flat*, Enfield, 1992.

Taylor, Arthur, *The Guinness Book of Traditional Pub Games*, London, 1992.

Thorne, Guy, *The Great Acceptance. The Life Story of FN Charrington*, London, 1913.

Thornett, Ken, (with Easton, Tom), *Tackling Rugby*, Melbourne, 1965.

Thrills, Adrian, *You're Not Singing Anymore*, London, 1998.

Tischler, Stephen, *Footballers and Businessmen*, New York, 1981.

Tranter, Neil, *Sport, Economy and Society in Britain 1750–1914*, Cambridge, 1998.

Tranter, N.L., 'The Cappielow Riot and the Composition and Behaviour of Soccer Crowds in Late Victorian Scotland', *International Journal of the History of Sport*, Vol. 12, No. 3, December 1995.

Tyneside Golf Club *Centenary 1879–1979*, Newcastle, 1979.

Vaizey, J.E., *The Brewing Industry, 1886–1951*, London, 1960.

Vamplew, W., *The Turf*, London, 1976.

——, 'Sports Crowd Disorder in Britain 1870–1914: Causes and Controls', *Journal of Sport History* , no. 7, 1980.

——, *Pay Up and Play the Game*, Cambridge, 1988.

——, 'Still Crazy After All Those Years: Continuity in a Changing Labour Market for Professional Jockeys', *British Journal of Contemporary History*, 14.2, Summer 2000.

Warner, Philip, *The Harlequins*, Derby, 1991.

Watts, Gerald, *Royal St Georges*, Sandwich, 1996.

Weir, John (ed.), *Drink, Religion and Scottish Football 1873–1900*, Renfrew, 1992.

Weir, R.B., 'The Drinks Trade' in R. Church (ed.) *The Dynamics of Victorian Business*, London, 1980.

Welcome, John, *Fred Archer: A Complete Study*, London, 1990.

Wentworth Day, J., *Inns of Sport*, London, 1949.

Wigglesworth, F.G., 'The Evolution of Guinness Advertising', *Journal of Advertising History*, 3, March 1980.

Wigglesworth, Neil, *The Evolution of English Sport*, London, 1996.

Williams, G.P., and Brake, G.T., *Drink in Great Britain, 1900–1979*, London, 1979.

Williams, G., *The Code War*, Harefield, 1994.

Williams, J.G.P., *Medical Aspects of Sport and Physical Fitness*, Oxford, 1965.

Williams, J., 'Churches, Sport and Identities in the North, 1900–1939' in Jeff Hill and Jack Williams (eds), *Sport and Identity in the North of England*, Keele, 1996.

Williams, Russ, *Football Babylon*, London, 1990.

Willock, Colin, *The Worthington Guide to Coarse Fishing*, Burton on Trent undated [c1965?].

Wilson, G.B., *Alcohol and the Nation*, London, 1940.

Wilson, R.G., *Greene King: A Business and Family History*, London, 1983.

Wootton, Steve, *Nutrition For Sport*, London, 1989.

Young, Percy M., *Bolton Wanderers*, London, 1961.

Unpublished Manuscripts

Baxter, J., 'The Organisation of the Brewing Industry', PhD thesis, University of London, 1945.

British Market Research Bureau Ltd, 'Licensed Premises. Report on an Attitude Survey', August 1960. Prepared for the Brewers' Society.

Clarke, I.D., 'The Origins and Development of Cricket in Cornwall until 1900', MA dissertation, De Montfort University, 2000.

Crellin, John Fynlo, '"The more things change, the more they stay the same": An analysis of how Saracens and Leicester Football Clubs have managed the transition from amateur sporting clubs to professional sports businesses', MA dissertation, De Montfort University, 1999.

Crowhurst, Andrew, 'The "Portly Grabbers of 75 per cent": Capital Investment and the Commercialisation of the British Entertainment Industry, 1885–1914', unpublished paper, 1999.

Dean, Alison, 'Merger Activity in the English Brewing Industry. 1945–1960: The Implications of being a Landlord', PhD thesis, University of Massachusetts, 1995.

Harvey, Adrian N., 'The Evolution of British Sporting Culture 1793–1850', D.Phil. thesis, Oxford University, 1995.

Hawkins, K., 'The Conduct and Development of the Brewing Industry in England and Wales 1880–1938', PhD thesis, University of Bradford, 1981.

Humphries, Tony, 'Regulation of Alcohol Advertising and Sports Sponsorship in the U.K.', paper presented to the ICAA Conference, Stockholm, June 1991.

Sportscan (Sports Sponsorship Computer Analysis Ltd), 'Analysis of Televised Sponsored Sport', London, 1982.

Stewart, Duncan, 'Alcohol: The Ethical Dilemma', MA dissertation, University of Warwick, 1997

Taylor, Matthew, '"Proud Preston": A History of the Football League, 1900–1939', PhD thesis, De Montfort University, 1997

Interviews

Micky Burns, Professional Footballers Association
Michael Caulfield, CEO, Jockeys Association
Gordon Taylor, CEO Professional Footballers Association
Michael Turner, Chief Medical Officer, Jockey Club

Index

Abbey Arms, 23
Abrahams, Alphonse, 94
Adams, Tony, 104, 112
Adidas, 111
Alcohol Concern, 103, 105, 124
alcohol
    advertising regulations, 59
        see also 'Beer is Best', Guinness
    as an aid to athletic training, 91–4
    as an aid to health, 49–50, 53, 92, 94
    calming effects of, 97
    opposition to athletes using, 93
    physical effects of, 95
    restrictions on its use, 98
alcoholism
    among footballers, 105
    among jockeys, 106–7
    in general population, 107
Alhambra Sports Club, 56
Allander Bowling Club, 28
Allerton Bywater, 19
Allied Breweries, 56, 61
Alpine Club, 40
American College of Sports Medicine,
    95
Angel Inn, 19
angling, 29
    in Scotland, 22–3
    clubs use of pubs, 31
Anheuser–Busch, 64
animal sports, 8
    decline of , 17
anti–Semitism
    and drink, 74–5
ape baiting, 8

Appleyard, Bill, 104
Archer, Fred, 97
archery, 97
    bans use of alcohol, 98
Army Council, 21
Arsenal FC, 99, 104, 109
Ashton, Brian, 111
Askeans RFC, 62
Aston Villa, 42, 46, 109
    supporters drinking before match,
        72–3
    use of private investigator, 109
Athletic News, 43
Atkinson, Ron, 96, 103, 109

Badcock, Jonathan, 91
badger baiting, 6
bagatelle, 31
Balls Pond Road
    derivation of name, 7
Bank House Inn, 21
Barclay Perkins, 42
Barclay, 'Captain', 91
Barclay's Bank, 55
Barnes, John, 112
Barnes, William, 108
Barnsley AFC, 46
Barnsley Bitter, 73
Barnsley, 22
Barry, Ron, 98
bars
    profits from, 72
Bass Brewers
    abandon brewing, 123
    advertising in 1930s, 51

bottled beer, 16
loans to clubs, 55
merge with Worthington, 33, 49
sponsorship of sport 59–61
sports provision for employees, 44
success of football sponsorship, 63, 65
take over Mitchells and Butlers, 56
Bat and Ball Inn, 10
Batley RLFC, 120
Batley RUFC, 55
Baxter, Jim, 104
Beamish, Charles, 41
Beamish, George, 41
bear–baiting, 7
Beasley, Bobby, 105
Beer Act (1830), 10
Beer and Skittles, 43
'Beer is Best' advertising campaign,
   49–51
Beer Orders, 122–3
beer
   as aid to training, 91, 94
   bottled, 16, 31
      at football matches 71–2
      banned from grounds, 84
   canned, 56
      banned from grounds, 84
   fall in consumption, 15, 31, 49, 56
Begleiter, Henri, 105
Belcher, Jem, 9
Belfast Temperance League, 58
Bell's Life in London, 91
Bell's whisky, 63
Bennett, Mark, 103
Benskin's Brewery, 47
Bentley, J.J., 47
Best, George, 99, 104
Betting Houses Act (1853), 11
Billiard Table Makers' Association, 27
billiards, 25–6, 31, 120, 121
Birmingham and District Cricket
   League, 41
Birmingham and District Works Cup, 57

Birmingham St George's
   see Mitchell St George's
Birmingham, 9, 27
   pub conversations in, 24
Black & White whisky, 25, 52–3
Black Bull Hotel, 28
Black Bull Inn, 23
Blackburn Rovers, 13–14
Blakeborough, J. Fairfax, 29
Blakeney's Head, 9
Blue House Inn, 12
Bo'ness, 22
Bollinger, 59
Bolton Wanderers FC, 81, 107
   1946 crowd disaster, 81
Bolton, 25
   Infirmary Cup (bowls), 29
   pub conversations in, 24
   women in local pubs, 33
Boon, David, 96
bottle parties, 82
Bourneville, 42
Bowling Green Inn, 7, 27
bowls, 5,6, 19
   growth of,16, 27–8
   in Scotland, 22, 27–8
   revival in 1970s, 62
   use of pubs, 31
boxing, 5, 8–9
   use of brandy in prize fights, 91–2
   debate over use of alcohol, 94
Boyce Hill Golf Club, 54
Bradford City AFC, 71
Braid, James, 103
Brailsford, Dennis, 9
brake clubs, 72
brandy, 91–2
breathalyser test for motorists, 77
Breckton, Marmaduke, 32
breweries
   financial support to football clubs,
      46–8
   sponsorship of sport, 57–65

sports provision for employees, 41–4
Brewers' Journal, 49
Brewers' Society, 49, 74
  advertising, 50–1, 54, 94
brewing industry
  consolidation in 1890s, 16
  economic problems of inter–war
    years, 49–50
  flotations, 14
  'merger mania' in 1960s, 56
Brickwood's, 15
Bristol, 43
British Medical Association, 124
Broughton Rangers RLFC, 12
Brown, J.T., 10, 108
Bruntsfield Links, 23
Budweiser, 124
Bull and Mouth
  derivation of name, 7
bull baiting, 6
Burnley, James, 24
Burton on Trent, 33
Butler, Frank, 97
Butterfield, Jeff, 96

Camanachd Cup, 63
Cameron, John, 104
Cannon, Tom, 92
Capper, W. Bently, 24, 30–1
Cappielow Riot 1899, 82
card games, in pubs, 30
Cardiff Arms Park, 76
Cardiff RFC 40–1
Cardigan Arms, 14
Carling lager 61, 63
Carlsberg, 61, 62
  success of football sponsorship, 63
Castle, The, 9
Caton, Tommy, 104
Cauthen, Steve, 105, 106
Celtic FC, 13, 82–3
  links with temperance, 120
Cemetery Tavern, 12

Chamberlain, Austen, 80
champagne, 45, 59, 92, 94
  aid to jockeys, 97
Chapel Allerton, 7
Charles II
  love of duck baiting, 8
Charlton Athletic AFC, 104
Chataway, Chris, 57
Chatham Civil Service Club, 54
Chelsea AFC, 84
Cheltenham racecourse, 70
  Gold Cup, 98, 105
Chester's Brewery, 47
Chesterfield, 70
cider, 60, 63
  aid to training, 91
Clarke, William, 10
clay pigeon shooting, 21
Clegg, Charles, 108, 120
clubs
  growth of, 16–7
  impact of drink–driving legislation,
    77
  impact on brewing methods, 51–2
  inter–war years 31–2, 51
  'middle–class pubs', 17
  'tied' status in inter–war years, 54
Cobbold's Brewery, 62
Coca Cola, 124
cock fighting, 6, 8, 11, 69
Cock Inn
  derivation of name, 6
coffee houses, 120
cognac, 92
Coleman, Thomas, 6
Colonel Bogey whisky, 45
Combe Delderfield, 39
Combe, Harvey, 39
Conservative party, 41
Corcoran, Peter, 9
corporate hospitality at sports grounds,
  79–80
Courage, 8

logo, 39
sponsorship of
  darts, 58
  quoits, 62
  rugby union, 62
  taken over by Imperial Tobacco, 61
Courage, Piers, 41
coursing, 18–20, 29
  decline of 32
Coventry City AFC, 72
Cowan, James, 110
Craven Heifer, 19
Crawshaw, E.H., 108
Cribb, Tom, 9
cricket, 5, 10
  brewers playing, 40
  drinking
    at matches, 77–9
    by players, 104, 106
    during matches, 93
    in league cricket, 101
  growth of clubs, 16–7
  National Village Cricket
    Championship, 59
  South African tours (1965), 59,
    (1970), 60
  sponsorship of, 59–60
  use of in advertising 51–2
Cricketer, 25
Crickets, 7
Crisp, Tom, 111
Crisp, Tom, 96
curling, 22
  sponsorship of, 63
Curtis, H.L., 92
Cutty Sark whisky, 60
cycling, 92

Daft, Richard, 40
Danish football fans (Roligans), 85
Darts Weekly News, 58
darts, 31
  alcohol as an aid, 97
  beer consumption in, 86

crowd behaviour, 86
growth of, 32–3
sponsored by breweries, 57–8, 61
Davies, J.H., 47
Department of Environment Working
  Group (1984), 72
Derby Arms
  derivation of name, 57
Derby Turn
  derivation of name, 57
Derby, 9
Derby, Earl of, 8, 57
Dettori, Frankie, 106
Dewar's Temperance Hotel, 120
dice, 30
Dillon, Bernard, 105
Dingle, A.E., 15
distillers
  sponsorship of sport, 62–3
Dog and Duck
  derivation of name, 7
dog fighting, 15
Doncaster Cup, 104
Dorchester, 40
Double Diamond, 69
Douglas Arms, 23
Douglas Hotel, 23
Dowling, Vincent, 91
Drake, Sir Francis, 27
Drinking and Public Disorder, 85
Drybrough, Andrew, brewer, 60, 63
Drysdale, William, 22
duck baiting, 8
Ducking Pond Mews
  derivation of name, 7
Dumbarton AFC, 100
Dunning, Eric, 85
Durham County Cricket Club, 96
Durham Ox Inn, 20
Durham, 27, 29

East Sheen Lawn Tennis Club, 52
Edgbaston cricket ground, 79
Egan, Pierce, 9

Elridge Piper, 40
Emmett, Tom, 10, 108
English Bowling Association, 22, 43
Eriksson, Sven–Goran, 111
Escott, T.H.S., 17
Ettingshausen, Andrew, 97
Evans, Alan, 96
Everton FC, 12, 46, 74

FA Cup, 46
    drinking at final, 71–2
    report on 1923 final, 81
    sponsorship of, 60–1
Fairfield Golf Club, 55
Fancy, The, 91
fencing, 97
    ban on use of alcohol, 98
Field, The, 102
Firearms Control Act (1920), 21
Fistiana, 9
Football Alliance, 42
football
    clubs
        growth of, 16
        shareholders of, 12–13
        Sunday football clubs, 34
        use of pubs, 11–12, 31
    hooliganism
        and alcohol, 80–7
        not caused by alcohol, 83
    identification with alcohol, 124
    in Scotland, 81
    players
        alcoholism among, 104
        become publicans when retired,
            112
        obtain jobs in pubs, 13–14
        stress leading to drink, 106
        women players and alcohol, 101
    undermines drinking, 15, 80
Football League Cup, 61
Football League, 107
    popularity of, 46

temperance links, 15, 108, 120
    Watney Cup, 60
Fordham, George, 104
Forfar Athletic AFC, 100
Foster's lager, 60
Fountain Inn, 9
Fox and Hounds
    derivation of name, 7
Fox Kilby, Kate, 85, 86
Francome, John, 106
Fulham AFC, 102

Gallacher, Hughie, 108
gambling
    in pubs, 19, 30
    opposition to, 70
Gaming Act (1845), 26
Gascoigne, Paul, 104
Gast, Margaret, 92
George, The, 9
George's Brewery, 43, 48
gin, 70, 93
    advertising of, 45
Giulianotti, Richard, 86
Glasgow Bowling Association, 22
Glasgow Celtic Society Cup, 63
Glasgow Evening Times, 19, 22–3
Glasgow Herald, 19
Glasgow
    bans games in pubs, 81, 122
Glenmorangie, 63
Gloucester, 27
Golf Blend Scotch, 45
golf
    advertising, 51, 52
    British Open, 59, 79
    clubs
        growth of, 17, 45
        importance of drinking to, 53,
            74–5
        links to brewers, 55
    corporate hospitality at, 79
    drunkenness in Victorian golf, 102–3

nineteenth hole
  derivation of term, 46
  importance to golf culture, 74
  in advertising, 52, 53
  sponsorship, 59
  in Scotland, 63
  see also anti–Semitism
Golf Illustrated, 45
Goring and Streatley Golf Club, 100
Gough, Harold, 121
Grand Caledonian Curling Club, 22
Grand National, 39
Grant's Morella Cherry Brandy, 44–5,
  94
Grant's Sloe Gin, 45
Grantham, 9
Graveney, Tom, 57
Graves, Henry, 30
Gray, George, 121
Greaves, Jimmy, 99, 104, 106, 107,
  109–10
Green, Canon Peter, 30
Greyhound Racing Association, 59
greyhounds, 29, 32
Grimsby Town, 42
Guinness, 54
  advertising campaigns, 49–51, 94
  Book of Records, 57
  flotation of, 14
  sponsorship of
    cricket, 60
    jockeys, 106

HP Bulmer, 60
Haig whisky, 52, 59
Halifax, 7
Hambledon Cricket Club, 10
Hancock, Ernest, 41
Hancock, Frank, 40–1
Hancock, Philip, 40–1
Handbook of Football, 15
Hansen, Alan, 112
Hare & Hounds, 7

Harlequins RFC, 75
Harp lager, 60
Harrison, Brian, 11, 29
Hart, Walter, 108, 120
Harvey, John, 45
Hastings, Scott, 111
Hazlitt, William, 9
Headingley stadium, 40, 60
  behaviour of cricket spectators, 79
Heart of Midlothian AFC, 46, 102,
  109
Heineken lager, 62
Hellesdon Golf Club, 55
Hendon Greyhound Track, 56
Henley Regatta, 71
Hennessey Brandy, 58
Hibernian AFC, 120
Hicks, Thomas, 92
Higgins, Mark, 12
Hills, Arnold,108, 121
Holroyd, Frank, 53
Holte, 72
Home Office Committee of Inquiry
  (1986), 80
Home Office Report into Crowd Safety
  (1986), 84
Hope, John, 120
Horse and Jockey, 7
Horse racing
  alcohol as an aid, 97, 98
  alcoholism among jockeys, 104–5
  crowd behaviour, 69–70, 86
  injuries to jockeys, 107
  see also Sandown Gold Cup,
    Simonds, Whitbread
Houlding, John, 12, 46
Huddersfield, 7
Hull and District Rugby Union, 45
Hull Brewery, 45
Hunslet RLFC, 12, 42
Hunter, Andrew, 22
Hunter, Ramsey, 103
hunting, 69, 100

Hurlingham, 21
Hussey, Bert, 52

identity
  beer and local, 73
  Scottish, 86
Ilford Golf Club, 54
Ilkeston, 20
Ind Coope, 49, merger with Tetley
  Walker, 56
India Pale Ale, 52
Indoor League (TV programme), 61
International Olympic Committee
  restrictions on alcohol, 98

J.D. Wetherspoon, 123
J. Lyons & Co., 61
Jockey Club, 98
jockeys
  see horse racing
Jockeys' Association, 107
Johanneson, Albert, 104
John Player Sunday League, 78
Johnny Walker whisky, 52
Jolly Brewer, 9
Jordan, Joe, 62

Kettering Town AFC, 96
Kilmarnock AFC, 12
Kilmarnock Silver Bowl, 22
King, Syd, 121
King's Lynn, AFC, 55
Knebworth, Viscount, 94
knur and spell, 18, 62
Krug champagne, 45

Lancashire County Cricket Club, 78–9,
  107
Lang Brothers, 63
Langer, Justin, 101
Law, Denis, 57
Lawrence, Gertrude, 51
Leamington RFC, 100

Lean, Michael, 106
Leeds Clarence Cricket Club, 40
Leeds Cricket, Football and Athletic
  Company, 40
Leeds St John's FC, 14
Leeds United AFC, 84
Lees, J.W., 46
  support for Oldham Athletic, 64
Lehman, R.C., 94
Leicester RFC, 77, 111
Leicester Town Crier, 16
Le Saux, Graeme, 112
Lewis, John, 15, 120
Liberal party, 41
Licensed Trade News, 5, 10, 94,121
Licensed Victualler, 26, 27, 71
Licensed Victuallers' Gazette, 30, 32
Licensing Act (1904), 16
Licensing Act (1961), 56
Licensing World, 21, 71, 121
Lincoln, 8
Lineker, Gary, 112
Liverpool FC, 12
  origins of, 46
  social drinking, 96
  sponsorship of, 61
  supporter's songs, 74
  TV advertising, 57
Liverpool, 9
  Chief Constable on drinking, 80
  ban on drinking on Saturday
    afternoons, 74
  ban on sports in pubs, 81, 122
Lloyd George, David, 48
Loates, Tommy, 104
Lockwood, Dicky, 14
Lockwood, William, 10, 108
London Breweries' Amateur Sports
  Association, 43
London Breweries' Football League, 43
London County Council, 28
London Irish RFC, 25, 41, 75
London Press Agency, 50

London, 9
    pub conversations in, 24
Lord, Thomas, 10
Lords' Taverners Cricket Club, 78
Lynch, Benny, 108

Macclesfield RUFC, 56
McCoy, Tony, 106
Macdonald & Muir distillers, 63
Macdonald, Malcolm, 111
McElhone Report (1977), 83
McEwan, William & Company, 111
    advertising, 45, 51
    sponsorship of golf, 63
McGrath, Paul, 109
Macgregor, William, 15, 108, 120
Mackeson Trophy, 59
madeira, 92
maggot racing, 62
Manchester Breweries, 47
Manchester City, 47, 104
    social club, 72
Manchester United, 47, 72, 99
    corporate hospitality, 80
    see also Newton Heath AFC
Manchester, 9, 56
Mangor, JP, 40
Marlow, Charles, 104
Marquis of Queensbury rules, 9
Marsh, Peter, 85
Martin, Skeets, 105
Martini, 59
masculinity
    beer advertising, 50, 124
    in the pub, 25
    local beer, 73
    rugby union, 75
Mass–Observation, 17, 24, 25, 31
    highlight popularity of darts, 33
    football supporters, 72, 81
Melbourne Breweries, 56
Mere Golf Club, 55
Merson, Paul, 99, 104, 106, 109–10

Metcalfe, Alan, 27
Methodism, 119
Middlesex County Cricket Club, 40
Miller, James, 15
Milligan, Spike, 25
Millwall AFC, 81
Milngavie West End Bowling Club, 23
Mitchell St George's FC 40, 42
Mitchell, Henry, 40, 42
Mitchells and Butlers, 13, 15
    advertising using sport, 41, 46, 57
    cricket team, 42
    sponsor bowls, 62
    support for West Bromwich Albion,
        46
    taken over by Bass, 56
    see also Mitchell St George's FC
modern pentathlon, 98
Moet et Chandon, 59
Molyneaux, Tom, 9
Moore, Bobby, 57
Morgan W.J., 76
Morgan, Robert, 23
Morse, Arthur, 40
Morse, Charles, 40
Morse, George, 40
motor racing, 41, sponsorship of, 59
Murrayfield, 76
Muscular Christianity, 119
music hall, 11

National Coaching Foundation, 99
National Coursing Club, 18
National Darts Association, 32
National Golf Clubs' Protection
    Association, 53
Nelson Inn, 18
Neville, Sidney, 50
Nevin, Pat, 96, 106, 109
New Inn, 27
Newcastle Breweries, 39
Newcastle Falcons RFC, 77
Newcastle United, 104

Newcastle, 28
Newport RFC, 40
News of the World, 32, sponsors darts, 58
Newton Heath AFC, 42, 47
    see also Manchester United
Nicholson, Bill, 109
Norfolk County Cricket Club, 40
Norfolk, 29
Norris, H.G., 102
Northampton Breweries, 46
Northern Union
    ban on players working as pub
        waiters, 14
    shareholders of clubs, 12–13
northernness
    and beer, 73
Northumberland, pigeon–shooting in,
    20
Norwich Speedway Company, 56
Nyren, John, 10

Odiham, Hampshire, 9
Old Trafford cricket ground, 79
Oldham Athletic AFC, 46, 64
O'Neill, Jonjo, 106
Oval Cricket Ground, 60
    popularity of drinking at, 78

Parkes, Tony, 96
Patrick Murphy, 85
Pearce, Henry, 104
Peel, Bobby, 10
Peel, Bobby, 93, 108
Pelican Arms, 27
Pepsi Cola, 124
Perry, William, 'The Tipton Slasher', 9
Phillips, Thomas, 40
pigeon shooting, 19–21, 32
Piggott, Lester, 97
Pike, Jim, 32
Place, Francis, 92
Plymouth, 27
polo, 59

Pompey, 15
Pontypridd RFC, 12
Port Glasgow F.C., 82
Port Vale AFC, 74
port, 93, 94, 100
Portland Group, 112
Portsmouth AFC, 15
Powell, Foster, 92
Preston North End, 45, 102
Prince of Wales
    abandons pigeon shooting, 21
*Principles of Training for Amateur
    Athletics*, 92
prints, used to decorate pubs, 29–30
prize fighting
    see boxing
Professional Footballers' Association,
    96, 104, 106, 110–11
Professional Golfers' Association, 122
PSV Hangover FC, 101
publicans
    decline in numbers brewing own
        beer, 16
    former sportsmen become, 9, 112
pubs
    competition from clubs, 17
    decline as a social centre, 123
    improvements to, 25–6
    music in, 11, 16
    names, 6–8
    opening hours restricted 1915, 30,
        48
    opposition to sports in, 26, 81
    rebranding in 1960s, 57
    reduction in numbers
        before 1915, 16
        during inter–war years, 31, 54
    signs, 6–8
    'tied' to breweries, 14–15, 16
    transformation into retail outlets, 61

Queen, 14
Queens Park FC, 102

Quinn, Mick, 103
quoits, 5, 23–4
  decline of 32
  revival, 62
  Scotland, 22–3
  violence in, 24

rabbit coursing, 15
Railway Hotel, 20
Rainbow, W.T., 26
Rainham Town AFC, 72
Ram Jam Inn, 9
Ramsey, Alf, 110
Randall, Jack, 9
Rangers FC, 72, 82–3, 104
rational recreation, 119
ratting, 8
Reading AFC, 47–8
Reading, 43
Real Ale Madrid FC, 101
Red Barrel
  see Watney's
Redruth Brewery, 40
Reed, Barras, 39
Reed, Bessie, 31
Rees, Leighton, 96
Reid's Brewery, 39
Rennie, John, 23
Richards, Dean, 111
Roberts, Robert, 6
Robinson, Fletcher, 120
Robson, Bobby, 103
rock climbing, 24
Root, Fred, 94, 100, 107
Rose's Lime Juice Liqueur, 45
rowing, 71, 94
Royal Academy, 54
Royal Caledonian Hunt Club, 100
Royal Commission on Licensing
  (1929), 27, 53, 54, 78
Royal Commission on Liquor Licensing
  Laws (1898), 80, 82
Rugby Football Union, 55

rugby league, 59
  Challenge Cup final, 72
  drinking and crowds, 86, 124
rugby union, 55, 120
  changes in culture due to
    professionalism, 77
  crowd disorder in, 86
  drinking culture of, 75–7, 92
    in women's rugby, 101
  sponsorship of, 62
  see also Welsh Rugby Union
rum, 92
running, 92

Sabbatarianism, 34
St Albans Turf Hotel, 6
Saint Monday, 5–6, 10
St Helens, 24, 32
Salford, 30
Samuel Smith's Brewery, 55
Sanders, Edgar, 49–50
Sandon Hotel, 12, 46
Sandown Gold Cup, 58
Scarborough Hotel, 13
Schweppes, 60
Scotch Whisky Association, 63
Scotland
  contrasts with England, 22, 23
  football fans change in behaviour, 86
Scotsman, 82
Scott, Bill, 104
Scottish and Newcastle Breweries, 62
Scottish Athletic Journal, 81, 93, 102
Scottish Bowling Association, 22, 27
Scottish Criminal Justice Act (1980), 83
Scottish Football Association, 120
Scottish F.A. Cup, 61, riot at 1909 final,
  82
Scottish Football Annual, 93
Scrumpy Jack cider, 60
Shearman, Montague, 93, 108
Sheffield United, 73
  stop selling alcohol at matches, 81

temperance policies, 121–2
Sheffield Wednesday, 42, 108–9
Sheffield, 9
sherry, 93, 96–7
shinty, 63
shooting, 69, 97
  ease of obtaining guns, 21
  restrictions on use, 32
  see also Firearms Control Act (1920),
    pigeon shooting
Simonds, H & G, brewers, 43–4, 49
  loans to supporters' clubs, 72
  purchase shares in Wembley, 55
  sponsor horse racing, 58
  support for Reading AFC, 47–8
Skittles, 5
Small Heath FC, 42, 108
Smethwick, 43
Smith, Doug
snooker, 25, 97, 105
social drinking, 95–6
Somerset County Cricket Club, 78
songs
  football songs about drinking, 73–4
South African Wines, 59
Southend Civil Service Sports Club, 54
Spalding's Football Annual, 104
Spanish Armada, 27
spirits
  as an aid to training, 91, 92
sponsorship of sport, 57–65
  see also corporate hospitality
Sporting Events (Control of Alcohol
  etc.) Act (1985), 80, 84
*Sports and Pastimes of the People of
  England*, 27
sports books
  produced by brewers, 57
sports company directors
  links with alcohol industry, 64
Sports Council (UK), restrictions on
  alcohol, 98
Sportscan, 63

Spring, Tom, 9
squash, 101
Squire, Ronald, 51
Star and Garter, 10
Stella Artois tournament, 62
Stephens, Stephen, 105
Steward and Patterson Brewery, 29, 40,
  73
Stewart, Duncan, 101, 111
Stewart, Ernest, 23
Stewart, V.C., 82
Stirling and District Quoiting
  Association, 23
Stirling Innkeepers' Stakes, 6
Stirling Races, 6
Stonehenge, 99
Stow's Survey, 8
Streatham Park Bowling Club, 55
stress, 106
Strutt, Joseph, 27
strychnine
  used with brandy as a stimulant, 92
Studd, C.T., 71
Sullivan, John, 108
Sun, 86
Sunderland AFC, 12, 14
Sutcliffe, Charles, 15, 108, 120
Swansea, 76
swimming, 94
Swinburn, Walter, 105, 106
Swindon Town AFC, 71
Swinton RLFC, 12

Talbot
  derivation of name, 7
Tartan Army, 86
Tattenham Corner, 57
Taylor Report on the Hillsborough
  Stadium Disaster (1990), 81, 85
Taylor Walker Breweries, 58
teetotallers, 106
  see also temperance
television commercials, 57

temperance
  angling in Scotland and, 23
  attempts to develop non–alcoholic
    sporting alternatives, 120–2
  ban on alcohol in Liverpool, 74
  campaigners in Football League
    leadership, 108, 120
  opposition to
    alcohol use by athletes, 93
    beer advertising, 50
    drinking at football matches, 71
    sport, 69, 119
  support darts, 58
Temperance Herald, 121
Tennant, John & Robert, brewers, 56
  sponsor
    Scotland world cup team, 58–9
    Scottish F.A. Cup, 61
tennis, 5, 16
  corporate hospitality, 79
  growth of, 17, 45
  sponsorship of, 62
Tetley Walker Breweries, 56
Tetley, C.F., 40
Tetley, Joshua & Son
  advertising, 44
  approached for loans, 55
  employee cricket club, 41
  sponsorships of sport, 60–2, 79
  sports facilities, 43
  takeovers and mergers, 56
  use of logo, 39–40
Thatcher, Margaret, 87
Thomas, Mickey, 106
Thomson's Weekly News, 104
Thorner, Graham, 106
Thornett, Ken, 99
Thornton Heath Sports Club, 54
Thurlow Arms, 26
Tipton Slasher, see Perry, William
Tipton, 9
tobacco
  competitor with alcohol, 15

consumption increase in inter–war
    years, 31
  sports sponsorship, 58
Tottenham Hotspur AFC, 12, 96, 109
  corporate hospitality, 80
  crowd, 71, 74
  hard–drinking reputation, 110
  supporters club, 54, 72
traditional sports
  survival of in pubs, 18–20
  revived in 1970s, 61
Trent Bridge cricket ground, 79
Trent Bridge Inn, 10, 40
Trueman, Fred, 57
Truman, John, 20
Truman's Brewery, 40, 56
  loans to clubs, 54–5, 72
  sports provision for employees, 43
  sports sponsorship, 59
Turner, Michael, 98
Twickenham, 76–7
Tyneside Golf Club, 74

Union Arms, 9
Uttoxeter racecourse, 70, 98

Vardon, Harry, 103
Varsity match, 76–7
Vaux, 62
VOB whisky, 52
Voltigeur, 104

Wainwright, Andy, 112
Wakefield Trinity RLFC, 109
Wakefield, 18
Wales
  brewers links with sport, 40–1
  'drink problem' in rugby union, 76
Walker Cain Breweries, 56
Walker, Billy, 57
Walker, V.E. 40
Ward, Jem, 92
Warner, P.F., 94

Waterloo Cup, 18
Watford AFC, 47
Watney Cup, 60
Watney's, 49, 97
   publish sports books, 57
   Red Barrel beer, 52
   sponsorship of
      darts, 61
      football, 60
   sports provision for employees, 43
   TV advertising, 57
Webster's Brewery, 62
Welsh Rugby Union
   ban on alcohol at internationals, 76
Welsh, Irvine, 86
Wembley stadium, 55
   report on 1923 final, 81
West Bromwich Albion AFC, 15, 42
   dependent on loans from brewery, 46
West Ham United AFC, 84, 108, 109
   hard–drinking reputation, 110
   temperance policies of, 121
Westerton Arms, 27
whisky, 52, 103
   advertising of, 45
   in Scotland 62–3, 70, 100
Whitbread, 14, 15, 39, 50
   abandon brewing, 123
   merger with Tennant's, 56
   sports sponsorships, 58, 59, 62
   see also Mackeson Trophy, Stella
      Artois tournament
Whitbread, Bill, 39
White Hart Inn, 12, 14, 15
White, Jimmy, 105
Wigram, William, 39

Williams, John, 85
Wilson, Jimmy, 102
Windsor Racecourse, 58
wine, 52, 59, 93, 94
Wolverhampton Wanderers AFC, 46
women
   and bowls, 28
   drinking in women's rugby and
      football, 101
   in pubs, 25
   popularity of darts among 32–3
   unwanted in rugby union clubs, 75
   see also masculinity
Woodhouse FC, 12
Working Party on Crowd Behaviour at
   Football Matches, 82–3
Worthington Cup, 61
Worthington, 33, 54
   merger with Bass, 49
   publish sports books, 57
   sponsor Football League Cup, 61
   sports provision for employees, 43–4
wrestling, 5

yachting, 59
Yorkshire Church Temperance, Shield,
   120, 122
Yorkshire Post, 18–19
Yorkshire TV, 61
Younger, William and Co. Brewers
   advertising campaigns, 51
   bottled beer, 16
   interest in Heart of Midlothian AFC,
      46
   links with clubs, 56
   sports provision for employees, 43